BATTLEFIELD LOG:

Quang Tri Province, January 29, 1972

Captain Hugh Mills and his wingman in the other Cobra, Lieutenant Lew Brewer, remained at six thousand feet. They never took their eyes off Tim Knight and his door gunner, Specialist-5 Rip Smith, in the Loach searching for the downed Phantom crew. As the Loach was roaring along the stream bed, a hail of automatic-weapon fire suddenly poured out of the jungle. Knight hurled the tiny Loach to the right. His fast break pinpointed where the enemy fire came from. Mills and Brewer instantly rolled their awesome gunships over on their sides and plunged down, hurtling toward the jungle like a pair of angry eagles that had just seen their fledgling threatened.

Mills centered the target area in his reflector gunsight, selected rockets, and hit the firing button. A battery of rockets screamed from the pods on the Cobra's stubby wings, roaring like fiery arrows into the enemy positions.

Mills took careful aim and pressed the button to fire another salvo of rockets. He felt a horrible shuddering and realized instantly that he had a "hang fire" in the left outer rocket pod. The rockets hung in the pods with their fiery motors burning fiercely. Finally they leaped clear, but they had been "hung" long enough to rip off the back end of the rocket pod itself. The detached portion of the pod flew backward into the tail rotor and tore it off. The Cobra spun wildly to the right, its nose pointed down toward the jungle. . . .

Bantam Books in The Fighting Elite series

The Fighting Elite™

U.S. AIRBORNE

Ian Padden

BANTAM BOOKS
TORONTO · NEW YORK · LONDON · SYDNEY · AUCKLAND

THE FIGHTING ELITE™: U.S. AIRBORNE
A Bantam Book / December 1986

Produced by Bruck Communications, Inc.
157 West 57th Street, New York, NY 10019.
Cover photo courtesy U.S. Army
Inside photos courtesy D.A.V.A.

ISBN 0-553-26146-0

Published simultaneously in the United States and Canada

Bantam Books are published by Bantam Books, Inc. Its trademark, consisting of the words "Bantam Books" and the por-
trayal of a rooster, is Registered in U.S. Patent and Trademark
Office and in other countries. Marca Registrada. Bantam
Books, Inc., 666 Fifth Avenue, New York, New York 10103.

PRINTED IN THE UNITED STATES OF AMERICA

KR   0 9 8 7 6 5 4 3 2 1

Acknowledgments

Many thanks to Major Gayle D. Sams, USA, Public Affairs Office, 82nd Airborne Division, and to the Public Affairs Officers of the 101st Airborne Division (Air Assault), Headquarters, U.S. Army Aviation Center, Fort Rucker, Alabama; the 4th Airborne Training Battalion, Fort Benning, Georgia; and to the D.A.V.A. for their help with photographs.

Ian Padden

Acknowledgments

Contents

Foreword

When airborne soldiers or airborne operations are mentioned, most people immediately think of paratroopers. However, such thinking is not quite correct, and in this book the word *airborne* is used in its true sense to include parachute operations, helicopter operations, glider operations, and all airmobile operations.

Without aircraft and their pilots and crews, there would be no airborne or airmobile operations: it is for this reason that chapters have been included on army aviators and their aircraft.

1
BATTLEFIELD LOG:
Quang Tri Province,
January 29, 1972

Between Khe Sanh and the Laotian border to the west, Highway 9 winds its way through the dank and dense triple-canopy jungle. It is little more than a rough, wide trail for the most part, but the jungle on either side is so thick and difficult to penetrate that in this kind of terrain it deserves to be called a highway.

Highway 9 runs across the border into Laos to the town of Tchepone. From there it continues across to the extreme west of the country until it reaches the town of Savannakhet on the Mekong River. One of the main Vietcong and North Vietnamese supply and infiltration routes, part of the Ho Chi Minh trail, runs north and south to intersect Highway 9 between Tchepone and the South Vietnam border.

Late in 1971 and early in 1972, when the United States was phasing down its operations in Vietnam, the enemy blatantly used the highway to send troops and supplies into South Vietnam. Efforts to stop the enemy were restricted almost entirely to air strikes, unless the enemy was seen in large enough numbers to justify moving large numbers of assault troops into the area.

On the hot, sticky, humid afternoon of January 29, a hunter-killer team of helicopters from the 5th Cavalry of the 101st Airborne Division was conducting a "visual reconnaissance" (looking for something to shoot at) along the highway between Khe Sahn and the Laotian border. It was almost 1600 hours and the patrol had not located the enemy in any great number when they received the call for assistance from an Air Force Forward Air Controller operating within the area.

The controller, code named "Covey," was flying a fixed-wing OV-10 Bronco and had been directing a flight of F-4 Phantoms on an air strike against an enemy stronghold when one of the Phantoms was shot down. The pilot and his weapons-systems officer had ejected and had landed in the jungle near the enemy. Covey requested air cover to keep the enemy from getting to the crew until the Air Force rescue helicopters from Da Nang, the massive Sikorsky HH-53B "Jolly Green Giants," arrived on the scene.

Captain Hugh Mills was leading the 5th Cavalry hunter-killer team, code named "Charley Horse," and he readily agreed to assist the Forward Air Controller. He turned his team away from Highway 9 and headed for the area where the Phantom had crashed.

The Charley Horse team led by Mills was from D (Delta) Troop, 3rd Squadron of the 5th Cavalry, and was composed of two elements, one being the hunter-killer unit and the other being the extraction unit. The hunter-killer element was comprised of two AH-1G Cobra gunships and a small OH-6 Cayuse scout helicopter, while the extraction element was comprised of a Huey UH-1N. The two AH-1G Cobra gunships (often referred to as "Snakes") were armed with fifty-two 2.75-inch rockets, a 2000/4000-rounds-per-minute 7.62-mm minigun, and a 450-rounds-per-minute 40-mm grenade launcher.

The rockets were carried in four pods, two on either side of the fuselage, which were mounted on "stub wings" just behind the cockpit and were fired by the pilot from the backseat. The M-134 minigun and the M-5 grenade launcher were mounted side by side in the nose turret at the front of the Cobra and were operated by the copilot in the front seat.

The OH-6 Cayuse (more usually called a "Loach" because of its resemblance to the fish of that name) was armed with one pilot-operated forward firing minigun on the left side and a .50-caliber M-60 machine gun operated by the single crewman on the right side. The UH-1N (referred to as a "Slick" because of its uncluttered configuration) was armed with two door-mounted, crew-operated M-60 machine guns and carried a complement of heavily armed Rangers.

While the hunter-killers foraged around and engaged the enemy, the extraction Slick would keep well clear. In the event that one of the Cobras or the Loach got shot down, the remaining two hunter-killers would provide covering fire while the extraction Slick moved in and hovered over the downed craft. Ropes would then be lowered and the Rangers would immediately rappel down to set up a defensive perimeter around the craft while the crew of the stricken machine was hauled up to the Slick. Once this had been accomplished, the Rangers would be quickly hauled aboard and the Slick would pull away.

Flying at an altitude of about 6,000 feet, the team arrived in the general area of the downed Phantom, which was at the bottom of a small valley in an area of dense jungle. The Forward Air Controller informed Mills that he was now in radio contact with the Phantom crew. They had informed him that they were near a stream bed and that the trees in the area were between

250 and 290 feet high—quite normal for the region. The downed Phantom pilot had also informed the OV-10 crew that their parachutes were tangled in the top of the canopy and that it might be possible to see them from the air.

On hearing this, Mills led his team around at altitude and everyone scanned the top of the jungle canopy in an attempt to locate the parachutes. The team flew around the area for a short time but saw no sign of the parachutes. Mills then decided to send the Loach down on a low-level scouting sortie and instructed the OV-10 pilot to inform the Phantom crew to call him when they heard it getting close to their position. (Mills could not talk directly with the downed crew; all communications between the Charley Horse team had to be relayed through the Forward Air Controller in the OV-10.)

The Loach pilot, Warrant Officer Tim Knight, pitched his craft over on its side and rapidly spiraled down toward the jungle canopy. The helicopter pilots of the Loach scouts and Cobra gunships had learned from bitter experience in Vietnam that the safest way to get down from altitude in enemy-infested territory was to do it suddenly and quite violently. (A steady descent would make them extremely vulnerable to enemy small-arms fire.) Knight pulled the Loach out in straight-and-level flight within twenty feet of the tree tops and commenced a practiced search pattern at a fast-forward speed, backward and forward across the meandering stream bed.

After about ten minutes Knight called Mills and informed him that he had located an enemy base camp. He could see Vietcong running for cover at the sight of his Loach. Mills ordered him to ignore the enemy and continue to sweep until the Phantom crew was located. He noted the position of the enemy camp and decided that when the Phantom crew had been located, his team would return to wipe out the enemy camp.

Mills and his wingman in the other Cobra, Lieutenant Lew Brewer, remained at six thousand feet. They never took their eyes off Tim Knight and his door gunner, Specialist-5 Rip Smith, in the searching Loach. Some five minutes later, as the Loach was roaring along the stream bed, a hail of automatic-weapon fire poured out of the jungle. Knight immediately called that he was taking fire and hurled the tiny Loach to the right, away from the stream bed. His fast break to the right pinpointed the area where the enemy fire came from. Mills and Brewer instantly rolled their awesome gunships over on their sides and plunged down from six thousand feet, hurtling toward the jungle like a pair of angry eagles that had just seen their fledgling threatened.

Mills fixed his attention on the target area as he saw Knight pull the Loach away from his line of fire. He knew that the experienced Knight would not move too far away from the target area, perhaps two hundred feet, not much more, as he would want to get back into the stream-bed area as quickly as possible after the gunships' attack run. Mills also knew he did not have to concern himself with the Loach getting in his way: he and Tim Knight had worked together as a close-knit hunter-killer team before. Each knew almost instinctively where the other would be at any time during a battle. They could almost tell what was going on from the inflections in each other's voice.

As Mills's Cobra closed on the area where the Loach had taken fire, he centered the target area in his reflector gunsight, selected rockets, and hit the firing button. A battery of rockets screamed from the pods on the Cobra's stubby wings, roaring like fiery arrows into the enemy positions on the side of the stream.

Brewer, in the second Cobra, was close behind his leader. Both Cobras pitched up from their firing pass and leveled out at fifteen hundred feet in a sweeping turn. Knight immediately flew back over the stream bed and resumed his search even before the smoke from the Cobras' attack had cleared. Within minutes he began taking more fire from the side of the stream bed: he again broke hard to the right and started to pull clear as the Cobras rolled in to attack from fifteen hundred feet.

Mills took careful aim and pressed the button to fire another salvo of rockets. He felt a horrible shuddering in the Cobra and realized instantly that he had a "hang fire" in the left outer rocket pod. The rockets hung in the pods with their fiery motors burning fiercely. Finally they leaped clear, but they had been "hung" long enough to tear off the back end of the rocket pod itself. The detached portion of the pod immediately flew backward into the tail rotor and tore it off.

The Cobra spun wildly to the right, its nose pointed down toward the jungle. Mills reacted quickly. Shouting to his copilot, Warrant Officer John Bryant, that they were going down, he cut the throttle and jockeyed the controls until the nose came up. The Cobra stayed level as it spun around and around. Mills carefully watched the top of the trees as his machine descended. He knew that timing of his actions was now of the utmost importance. Waiting until the Cobra was almost on top of the trees, he hauled back on the cyclic control and cut the power.

The gunship stopped spinning and dropped onto the tree tops some 250 feet above the jungle floor. The whirling rotor blades caught the trees and sheared off, taking most of the main rotor hub with them. The fuselage rolled upside down, plunging through the triple canopy into the darkness of the fetid jungle floor. Branches and vines lashed the plummeting fuselage, tearing engine covers off the stricken craft as it descended. But the trees slowed the descent. As the fuselage landed, it rolled over onto its right side with a tremendous lurch.

Tim Knight had aborted his search for the Phantom pilots as he watched his flight leader's craft plunge into the jungle. He immediately swung the Loach over the hole in the canopy and brought his craft to a hover. The gunship had not caught fire. But Knight could see the inert bodies of Hugh Mills and John Bryant inside the Cobra.

Knight held the Loach at the hover over the downed Cobra, watching for signs of movement. He was convinced that Mills and Bryant were only unconscious: they looked unharmed, and the fuselage around the cockpit was still intact. Knight was well aware that he was taking a terrible risk as he was an easy target for enemy small-arms fire. But he stayed by the defenseless Cobra, his door gunner ready with his M-60 to cut down the first Vietcong that approached the downed craft. The extraction Slick with the Rangers on board was heading for the position. Meanwhile, the second Cobra circled overhead, waiting to pounce at the enemy approach.

Knight remained at the hover for almost five minutes. Still, he could not see any sign of movement. Pulling away to check for signs of approaching enemy, he smiled when he returned to the wrecked Cobra a few minutes later. Mills was standing beside the fuselage, holding the CAR-15 automatic rifle that he always carried in the cockpit. He had taken off his helmet and was wearing the dark blue, cowboy-style Stetson cavalry hat that he always wore when he was not flying.

Knight realized that Mills was somewhat dazed. He was not moving. Knight's door gunner, Rip Smith, pulled out his survival radio and gestured toward it. That seemed to bring Mills out of his daze. He found his own radio and started talking.

Mills informed Smith that his copilot, who was still in the aircraft, was badly injured with a suspected broken back and neck and was in considerable pain. Mills said he had a head injury and felt he would black out at any moment. He asked Smith to keep talking to him so he would stay conscious. Smith told him that the Slick was almost there. He did not think the Slick would have too much trouble getting down to them to lift them out. After a few minutes, Mills returned to the fuselage to check on the condition of Bryant.

The Slick arrived and hovered overhead. The rappelling ropes snaked down through the trees but their ends dangled short, some forty feet above the jungle floor. The Slick pilot moved his machine over about two hundred feet where the trees were shorter and dropped the ropes again. This time they reached the jungle floor with about a foot to spare. As the door gunners "hosed" down the surrounding area with their M-60s, the Rangers, none of whom had been in combat before, started to rappel down.

The first Ranger to hit the ground was the medic. He amazed everyone by descending the rope at lightning speed. But his rapid first descent from a helicopter was not intentional. When the other Rangers reached the ground they discovered that the medic had forgotten to double-wrap the rope around the snap link on his rappelling equipment. Unable to slow himself, he had free-rappelled all the way to the ground. The medic had lost his M-16 rifle on the way down and had been badly bruised as he crashed through the branches of the trees. However, he insisted on advancing to the wrecked Cobra. He thrashed through the jungle with his fellow Rangers and was the first man to reach Mills.

Several Rangers helped Mills extract the injured Bryant from the Cobra while the remainder fanned out in a defensive perimeter. One Ranger immediately made contact with the enemy and had to shoot his way back to the Cobra. The others formed a tight defensive perimeter and prepared for a stiff fight. It was obvious that they could not move the injured Bryant, and the ropes on the Slick could not reach them in their present position.

Mills, now almost fully recovered, talked to Brewer in the Cobra overhead. Their situation was beginning to look desperate. The enemy was closing in around them. Brewer replied that he had already talked to the Forward Air Controller in the Bronco: a second Air Force Jolly Green Giant with an escort of two Air Commando A-1 Skyraiders was already on the way. The first Jolly Green Giant had already arrived and located the downed Phantom crew with its sophisticated sensing equipment. It was now hauling them out of the jungle.

For the next thirty minutes tensions ran high in the small group as the men waited for the enemy to charge. Suddenly there was the explosion of a hand grenade, the first sign of enemy presence since the initial contact with the Ranger scout.

The explosion occurred about seventy feet away from the downed machine. Mills called in the second Cobra gunship and the Loach scout to offer some protective fire. But the request was canceled when Brewer informed him that the explosion was caused by a "Willie Peter" (white phosphorous) rocket that had been fired by the Forward Air Controller in the OV-10 as a marker for the Jolly Green Giant and its escort.

A few minutes later the massive HH-53 appeared overhead. The downwash from the massive rotor blades blew the cavalry hat off Mills's head. The side door on the helicopter opened and a medic climbed onto the "jungle penetrator," suspended from the helicopter's winch. Another crew member handed him a portable litter and the medic was lowered three hundred feet to the crashed Cobra.

Bryant was placed in the litter and hauled up into the helicopter. Mills was examined by the Air Force medic and informed that, because of his head injury, he would have to be taken up in the litter. The medic insisted that Mills could not ride the penetrator in case he suddenly became dizzy or blacked out. After removing some "sensitive" components from his wrecked Cobra, Mills climbed on the litter, now wearing his flight helmet and carrying his automatic rifle and the parts from the Cobra.

As Mills was being hauled up, enemy troops were seen moving toward their position. The Skyraiders hurtled in and began strafing the area around the remaining Rangers. As the rescue helicopter quickly lifted the Rangers out on the winch line, two at a time, the Skyraiders kept up their strafing attacks. When the last Rangers were on board, the Jolly Green Giant pilot, Captain Roger Colgrove, pulled the HH-53 away from the wrecked Cobra and headed straight for Da Nang with the badly injured Bryant. Colgrove had just performed his first rescue mission.

John Bryant did indeed have a broken back and neck. After a few weeks in the hospital at Da Nang he was taken back to the States. Captain Hugh Mills's injury was minor and he soon returned to action. When he finally left Vietnam, Mills had completed some two years in the country on two tours of duty. He had amassed over three thousand hours of combat flying time and had completed over one thousand missions. Twenty-five percent of his missions had been performed as a pilot of a Cobra gunship and seventy-five percent had been carried out in what was considered to be the most dangerous flying job in the entire Vietnam war, that of a pilot in the Aero Scouts, flying the Loach (OH-6 Cayuse).

Hugh Mills was shot down sixteen times before he was twenty-five years of age. He was awarded a total of ninety-five decorations including six Purple Hearts, five Distinguished Flying Crosses, sixty-six Air Medals, three Silver Stars, three Bronzed Stars with "V," six Air Medals with "V," the Army Commendation Medal, the Vietnamese Distinguished Flying Cross of Gallantry with Silver Star, the Vietnamese Medal of Honor, the Vietnam Service Medal, and the Vietnam Campaign Ribbon. Hugh Mills was indeed a warrior of the air.

U.S. AIRBORNE

2
BATTLEFIELD LOG:
Normandy, June 6, 1944

Perhaps the primary practical requirement for the success of any airborne assault lies in the hands of the pilots flying the aircraft that transport the paratroopers to the drop zone. Two words, timing and accuracy, are the key to the successful start of any airborne assault. Both are vital to the success of the entire operation, particularly if it is a combined operation and set objectives must be met to assist the advancement of other assault units.

If the pilots of the transporters do not get the air-assault troops exactly on their designated drop zone on time, then the soldiers are burdened with the additional task of getting to their assigned target areas on foot. In enemy-occupied territory, that invariably means fighting their way to the drop zone. Any delay or inaccuracy of a "drop" negates the element of surprise and allows the enemy to better prepare itself to repel the attackers, thus making life even more difficult for the airborne assault unit.

All these factors were well known to the planners of the airborne-assault portion of the Normandy invasion. Because of their fears, the concerned planners saw to it that the transport pilots carrying the airborne units were well informed about the need for accuracy and control. In fact, the planners made a nuisance of themselves in their briefings with the pilots who would carry both the 82nd and 101st Airborne Divisions into France.

But the preparations were to no avail. Bad weather, heavy enemy antiaircraft fire, and bad navigation resulted in both Airborne Divisions being dropped in darkness over a fifty-square-mile area instead of an eight-square-mile area.

Staff Sergeant Harrison Summers of the 101st Airborne Division jumped out of a C-47 traveling at 180 miles per hour some five hundred feet above the ground. Although he had experienced some bad jumps in his two-year career in the Airborne, that jump was the worst ever. For days to come he would feel the bruises on his body where his parachute harness had almost crushed him. The canopy had deployed with a fierce crack in the screaming slipstream.

The pilot of the aircraft had been frantically trying to avoid enemy flak, and other troop-laden C-47s in the dark stormy skies above Normandy, when he broke out of a cloud bank and spotted the flare-type markers laid out by the pathfinders. He hastily told the troops to jump, and the Airborne men did not have to be told twice, as they just wanted to get out of the bucking and twisting, flak-riddled aircraft.

Summers landed in a muddy field. Once he had removed his parachute and picked up his pack, he set out to look for the rest of the men in his platoon. After searching around for a short time he made contact with several men from other platoons and squads but did not come into contact with any of his own men. Other soldiers, like Summers, had become separated from their own units in the total confusion of the drop.

Eventually the tiny group made contact with a larger party led by Lieutenant Colonel Pat Cassidy, the commander of the 1st Battalion. Accompanying him was Captain Frank Lillyman, leader of the pathfinder group that had dropped several hours before the main force to mark the landing zones. Cassidy and Lillyman had met shortly after Cassidy had landed, and they were now aware of the fact that the Airborne drop had been a disaster. The entire 101st Division, as well as the 82nd Division, was spread out all over the Normandy peninsula.

However, every man in the 101st had been fully informed that their mission was to clear the way for the 4th Infantry Division, which the Navy was to land on the coast at dawn in the area designated "Utah Beach." Cassidy believed that the scattered Airborne would have time to regroup and get to their assigned areas. But it would take extraordinary effort.

Cassidy knew he was just half a mile south of the town of Foucarville and a short distance from one of the division's primary targets—a large, four-gun German coastal artillery unit and barracks complex at Varreville. His group was steadily growing in size, with men straggling in from every direction, and Cassidy decided to set up a command post. When he established the post, he sent Captain Lillyman to set up a roadblock and ambush point near Foucarville while he led an attack on one section of the German barracks near the Varreville gun position.

The attack was an anticlimax. The first building the troops charged was empty. Cassidy immediately commandeered it for a command post, then sent out one group of men to take the remainder of the artillery-barracks complex and smaller groups to complete another part of his own battalion's mission of setting up roadblocks to hinder enemy reinforcements being rushed to the landing beaches.

Cassidy was told that massive four-gun battery had already been knocked out by Air Force bombers. At the gun position he found a small group from the 2nd Battalion, led by their commander, Lieutenant Colonel Steve Chappuis. Chappuis and his battalion had been fortunate enough to stay together for the air drop, but they had landed miles away from their primary target, the gun battery he was now standing on. So Chappuis selected twelve men and led them at high speed to Varreville while the remainder of his battalion followed at a more reasonable pace. As the battery had been destroyed, the disaster of the drop did not seriously affect the first part of the 2nd's operation. Chappuis informed Cassidy that he would remain at the gun position until the rest of his battalion arrived.

Returning to his own command post, Cassidy discovered that in his absence the troops he had sent to take the remainder of the artillery barracks were having problems. Their first attempt had failed as they encountered withering enemy machine-gun fire. Though Cassidy had very few men available, he sent as many as possible out to set up roadblocks, retaining only a handful to defend his command post.

When a few more men arrived, he felt it was worth risking a small unit to assist in taking the remainder of the German barracks. He could allocate only fifteen men, which he knew was not enough, but that was all he could spare. Staff Sergeant Summers would lead the group. Cassidy knew that Summers was calm and professional, and that it would take a good leader to handle a group that was a conglomerate of soldiers from different units.

Summers was not too happy about the idea. Not only

had he not worked with any of the men he had been assigned to lead, but most of the soldiers in the team did not even know one another. Experience had proved to Summers that, under fire, teamwork was essential for the success of any operation. He knew it was impossible to get this group acting like a team at such short notice.

As they left the command post and skirted around the hedgerows and stone walls of the area toward the barracks, the team was shot at several times. From the reactions of his mixed group, Summers decided that he would have to lead them by pure example—if he did not get shot down before they reached the target area. As he neared the first building of the barracks complex, he heard heavy firing. As he got closer, he saw several groups of soldiers pinned down by enemy fire that came from a row of stone buildings.

The enemy had cut narrow slits in the stonework of the buildings, enabling them to fire almost with impunity at the Airborne soldiers, who were now scattered behind walls, ditches, and hedgegrows. Summers saw a door at the side of the first building. He decided he might stand a slight chance of getting to the door without getting too badly hit. When he informed his men, their expressions told him more clearly than words that they were reluctant to be part of such an escapade.

Without attempting to persuade them, Summers crawled forward a short distance, checked his Thompson submachine gun, then broke cover. He raced toward the building, weaving from side to side as a hail of fire spattered around him. Approaching the door at full speed, he swung his foot up and smashed it open.

The room was occupied by nine enemy gunners, who were firing out through slits. The Germans swung around just as Summers swung his tommy gun up to fire. Several of the enemy raced for the back door as one opened fire. Summers sidestepped quickly and opened fire with the tommy gun, killing four. As they fell, he swung in the direction of the back door just as the remainder of the enemy went through. But he was too late, and he made no attempt to pursue.

His men were still lying in the ditch on the other side of the road that ran past the buildings. They saw Summers reappear from the building, casually reloading his tommy gun. Summers glanced in their direction, then began crawling through a small hedge toward an adjoining building. His own men, as well as several other groups of pinned-down Airborne soldiers, watched in fascination as he charged through the door of the second building with the tommy gun blazing. A moment later, Summers stopped firing. A quick search confirmed that the building was empty. He came back out and again looked toward the ditch where his men were hidden. As he started toward the next building in the row, German machine gunners and snipers opened fire on him.

Private William Burt decided that his sergeant needed help. He scrambled up from the ditch, ignoring enemy fire as he set up his Browning automatic rifle. He brought the gun into action, concentrating on the slits of the third building. Burt was extremely accurate with the Browning. His shooting broke up the concentrated fire that pursued Summers.

Summers smiled. He was getting some help from his own men at last. As enemy fire decreased, he charged the door of the third house. He received some unexpected company: Lieutenant Elmer Brandenberger.

The lieutenant, who was from Summers's company, had been with one of the original groups that had been sent to take the barracks, but he had been pinned down by the enemy gunners until Burt had forced the enemy to keep their heads down. With the easing of the enemy fire, Brandenberger sprang from cover to assist the sergeant.

Summers was pleased for the help, but it did not last long. Brandenberger was hit by a blast of machine-gun fire as he raced toward the door of the building. Hurled to the ground by the impact of the bullets, Brandenberger was severely wounded.

Without slowing down, Summers hit the door and crashed into the building. A swirl of enemy uniforms caught the fire from the bucking tommy gun in his hands. Three men fell dead. Another three went for the door, but they never made it. They were cut down in the sweep of Summers's tommy gun.

Pausing at the door, Summers reloaded the tommy gun. He saw a medic pulling Brandenberger to safety. Taking a deep breath, he stepped outside. Burt started firing again to give him cover as Summers turned toward the fourth building.

He was joined by a captain wearing the shoulder patches of the 82nd Airborne. Just as Summers registered the insignia, the captain dropped, felled by a German sniper.

Summers shook his head. Booting down the door of the fourth house, he leaped inside with the submachine gun kicking in his hands. Five enemy soldiers fell to the floor without firing a shot. The sixth went down as he leveled his Schmeisser submachine gun at Summers.

Private John Camien, lying in the ditch behind Burt and his machine gun, saw the 82nd Airborne captain fall. His newly acquired sergeant was on his own again. Picking up his M-1 rifle and some spare ammunition for the tommy gun, Camien shouted to Burt and the remainder of the men to give him covering fire. He set off at a run across the road and down along the row of buildings. Despite the covering fire, a fusillade of enemy bullets ricocheted off the building walls and tore at the ground beneath Camien's feet.

As he reached the door of the fourth house, Camien almost collided with Summers, who was just coming out. A smile appeared on Summers's grease-blackened and sweat-stained face.

Summers led the way to the next building. One tremendous blow from his boot took the door off its hinges. Camien flattened against the outside wall as enemy gun flashes burst past him. Summers, meanwhile, engaged in a duel with five enemy soldiers inside the room. When smoke and dust settled, Summers was the only one left standing.

Camien stepped inside and waited for Summers to reload the tommy gun before reloading his own carbine. Then Summers exchanged his tommy gun for the carbine, telling Camien to go ahead and take the next building.

As the two men broke out the door, Burt again provided some covering fire. Camien thrashed through a small hedge, with Summers right behind him. Camien hit the door and burst inside the building as the shattered door hit the floor. Standing almost in the middle of the room, Camien swept it with an arc of fire from the tommy gun, and five enemy soldiers went down.

Summers stepped inside quickly and they exchanged weapons again. Both of them caught their breath for a few moments before dashing out into the open and heading for the next building. When Summers's first assault on the door did not break it down, he hosed it with fire and kicked it, splintering, into the room.

The six enemy soldiers inside the building were

waiting for him, but to no avail. They paused for a fraction of a second and Summers gunned them down with one sweeping burst.

Again Summers and Camien exchanged weapons and started out the door, but a torrent of enemy machine-gun fire forced them back inside. The enemy machine gunners poured fire through the open door, tearing into the dead bodies of their own men in the room. Summers heard Burt start up with the Browning and a few moments later the enemy fire stopped amid the agonizing screams of the wounded. One deadly accurate burst from Burt's Browning was enough to put the enemy gun out of action.

After the short delay, the two men took off toward the next building. Camien went through the door in a more controlled manner and instantly killed the first two enemy soldiers who appeared. As he went farther inside, another four enemy soldiers pulled back from the slits in the wall: Camien gunned them down before they could aim their weapons.

Summers came inside quickly and informed Camien that the next building was the last in the row. Most of the firing outside now seemed to be an exchange between that building and Burt's Browning. Camien hastily reloaded the Thompson and returned it to Summers. They charged out the door and made for the last building in the row.

The door crumpled easily beneath Summers's boot. Six more enemy were dead within seconds as Summers swung the rattling tommy gun left and right around the room. As he came inside, Camien observed that there was now almost no enemy fire. Even Burt could find nothing to shoot at.

When he had reloaded the submachine gun, Summers went to one of the slits at the end of the room and

peered out. Past the end of the row of buildings that he
and Camien had just cleared he could see a long, low
building. He thought he saw someone going inside
through a door at one end. Signaling Camien to follow,
Summers carefully made his way toward the building. A
few shots were fired in their direction, but Summers
assumed the shots came from a sniper hidden somewhere at their flank.

Burt, who had again repositioned his Browning, started
to fire short bursts in the direction of the sniper as
Summers raced for the side door of the low building.

The door burst open and Summers leaped inside. It
was a large room. Fifteen German soldiers were calmly
eating breakfast as if completely unaware that they
were in the middle of firefight. Summers held his fire
as he considered taking them prisoner. Had they remained
seated, they would almost certainly have lived to see
the end of the war.

But their destinies changed in that split second when,
almost as one, they went for their weapons. Summers
let fly with the tommy gun, releasing the trigger only
when he was out of ammunition. As his gun clicked on
empty, he roared for Camien to assist him. But there
was no need. All the enemy had fallen beneath the
raging Thompson machine gun. None was still alive.

When Summers and Camien came out of the building they were met by Burt, the remainder of the
original fifteen-man unit, and a few dozen others. A
young lieutenant informed Summers that there was one
large, double-story building a short distance away that
was being heavily defended by perhaps a hundred
enemy soldiers. Lieutenant Colonel Cassidy was bringing up some reinforcements to clear it out.

Summers led his men toward the building through a
series of ditches and hedgerows. The hedges stopped a

short distance from the building. A flat, open field lay in front of them. Summers ordered the men in his group, now somewhat reinforced and led by the newly arrived lieutenant, to deploy along the hedgerow. As they did so, a sniper started to shoot and several men were hit. The lieutenant ordered an attack. The group started across the field but was driven back by heavy enemy fire. Four men were killed, including the lieutenant, and several were badly wounded.

Summers noticed a wooden shed alongside the building and, beside that, a large haystack. He called the marksman Burt and asked him if he could set it on fire with tracer rounds. Burt eagerly obliged. The haystack went up in flames. Just as Summers had hoped, the wooden shed also caught fire, but what occurred next was much more than he had hoped for. The shed erupted in explosions. The enemy had been using it to store ammunition for the now-useless coastal guns.

As enemy soldiers ran from the shed and from the edge of the large building, the Airborne soldiers cut them down. Moments later, Sergeant Roy Nickrent, carrying a bazooka, appeared beside Summers. The two sergeants decided that they would attempt to penetrate the thick stone walls of the building, but the roof might be vulnerable. Nickrent used a few rounds to get his aim in and then started to place rounds squarely on the roof. After several rounds had landed, enemy soldiers started to flee from the building in great numbers. Summers's men, on the south side of the building, cut down all those who came within their sights, but a large group broke for the north and west. Those headed north ran straight into the leading units of the 4th Infantry Division that had just come up along the roads protected by Cassidy's men. The enemy that ran west were just as unfortunate: they met a large group of Airborne troops led by Lieutenant Colonel John Michaelis.

The three groups killed some fifty men and took thirty as prisoners. Summers seized control of the large building.

During the entire encounter, Staff Sergeant Harrison Summers had wiped out fifty of the enemy. Private Camien had killed eleven.

For his gallantry and leadership in the field of battle, Staff Sergeant Harrison Summers was awarded a battle-field commission and the Distinguished Service Cross. Despite the confusions caused by the terrible air drop, he had assumed the responsibilities of control and leadership when both were needed.

As to the over-all consequences of the scattered air drop over Normandy, acts of valor and leadership predominated. Fate, or perhaps luck, lent a helping hand. Although the Airborne units were somewhat confused when they first landed, the German high command was even more confused by the reports of parachutists landing over such a large area. As a result, the Germans decided not to deploy their reserve troops and other reinforcements until they could work out what the Allies were trying to do. Their delay allowed the Airborne troops to regroup and the Allied Infantry to advance far enough inland to establish a firm hold in France. Ultimately, this blunder cost the German high command the entire war.

3
Arms and Fighting Equipment (Airborne and Air Mobile)

Modern airborne and air mobile units have a wide variety of specialized weaponry and equipment available to them, and a considerable amount of it has been well tried and proven in battles in Vietnam, Lebanon, and Grenada. This chapter gives a brief description of some of the major weapons and equipment currently in use and also describes some new equipment that has just entered service with both airborne and air mobile units.

Small Arms

The basic weapon of the airborne soldier is still the rifle. The one presently in service is the M-16A1, usually referred to as the M-16.

It is a 5.56-mm (about .22 caliber), magazine-fed, gas-operated, air-cooled weapon, and is perhaps one of the finest examples of a high-quality, mass-produced weapon. The aluminum magazine holds 30 rounds. The total weight of a fully loaded weapon, including the carrying sling, is just 8 pounds. An M-7 bayonet-knife can be mounted by attaching it to a stud directly below the front sight assembly.

Absolute maximum range is about 3,000 yards, and even at that range a 5.56-mm round can kill a human being if it strikes the head. Maximum effective killing range is about 500 yards, assuming the round hits a vital part of the body.

The M-16 was chosen as the U.S. Infantry weapon because it is lightweight, accurate, has a good range and killing potential, and because it has both automatic and semiautomatic fire capability—either of which can be chosen by simply moving a small selector lever.

M-203 Grenade Launcher

The 40-mm M-203 is a lightweight, single-shot, breech-loaded, pump-action, shoulder-fired weapon. It is attached to the barrel of a slightly modified M-16 rifle and does not interfere with the normal function of the rifle. The grenade launcher has its own trigger mechanism just forward of the rifle magazine. A special set of sights is attached to the top of the rifle.

The maximum effective range for the launcher is about 370 yards; for a point target, the range is closer to 160 yards. During combat the weapon can be fired quite safely at targets as close as 40 yards.

The M-203 is a versatile and highly effective weapon when used correctly. It has more types of rounds available than any other single-case weapon in the Army inventory. Further types are continually being developed to give the infantryman more diversified fire-power capability.

M-60 Machine Gun

The M-60 is a 7.62-mm, belt-fed, gas-operated, air-cooled, fully automatic weapon. The 7.62-mm rounds are fed into the gun by means of a disintegrating, metallic, split-link belt. The individual links of the belt are stripped off by the breech mechanism as each round is fed into the chambered barrel and fired. Expanding gases from the fired rounds drive the bullets through the barrel and also provide the necessary energy to operate the high-speed reload-and-fire mechanism.

Although the M-60 weighs only 23 pounds, a two-man crew operates the weapon—one to fire and one to feed the links of ammunition into the gun. The second man is also needed to carry spare equipment and ammunition, and occasionally a third man will be assigned to the crew in order to transport additional ammunition.

The maximum effective range of the M-60 is about 1,000 yards, but the weapon is deadly up to about 4,000 yards. The weapon is very popular with Airborne troops because of its light weight, accuracy, and tremendous fire power—about 550 rounds per minute.

M-249 Light Machine Gun

The M-249, now entering service with the Army, is being supplied to Airborne units. It is a 5.56-mm, magazine-fed, automatic weapon that is intended to complement traditional fighting squads and will not replace either the M-16 or the M-60.

The loaded weapon, with a 200-round magazine, is 1 pound lighter than an empty M-60 and has a rate of fire of some 750 rounds per minute.

It is a highly accurate weapon. At present, there are plans to supply one man in each squad with an M-249 to increase the squad's over-all fire power.

The M-249 is considered to be the most superior light machine gun in the world both in operation and in "knock down" power. Its M-855 ball ammunition can penetrate a traditional steel helmet at a range of 1,400 yards.

M-67 Hand Grenade

The hand grenade is one of the oldest types of weapons used by the American fighting man. Its use, in one form or another, in other parts of the world, dates back to about 1000 A.D.

The standard hand grenade presently used by Airborne units is the M-67 fragmentation grenade. It weighs approximately 14 ounces, has a smooth metal outer body, and is shaped like a small ball. The grenade is filled with 6.5 ounces of explosive material, known as Composition B, and the inside of the case is lined with a tight coil of serrated wire. When the pin is pulled (it is almost impossible to pull with one's teeth) and the grenade is thrown, the spring-loaded lever on the side of the grenade flies off and releases a plunger that strikes a detonating fuse. This time-delay fuse then detonates the Composition B, which explodes and hurls the fragmented body of the grenade and the serrated wire in all directions.

The casualty radius of the M-67 is about 15 yards. An average soldier can throw it about 40 to 50 yards.

M-1911A1 Pistol

The .45-caliber pistol—or sidearm, as it is more affectionately called—is really a last-resort weapon that is only effective up to about 50 yards, although it has a stated maximum range of 1,500 yards.

The current-issue sidearm (which has been in service for many years) is the M-1911A1, .45-caliber pistol. It is a recoil-operated, magazine-fed weapon with a capacity of 7 rounds, and every infantryman is taught how to use it. Amid great controversy, much of which is perhaps sentimental, the "faithful" old .45 automatic is about to be replaced with a more modern 9-mm pistol. (The 9-mm is almost a standard ammunition-size pistol among our allies and throughout the world's armed forces.)

MORTARS

M-224 60-mm and M-29A1 81-mm Mortars

The mortar has long been the bombardment weapon of the infantry, since it is fairly easily transported and is capable of accurately placing shells into close-range enemy positions—something that can be quite difficult for traditional artillery to do without endangering its own forces. The mortar is a muzzle-loaded weapon. It is mounted with the use of bipod legs and a base plate. The bottom of the barrel, or breech, is attached to the base plate, and when it is set up, the complete unit is actually a tripod, with the barrel acting as the third leg.

One of the characteristics of the mortar is that it is simple to operate. It can be set for either "drop fire" or "lever fire." In the drop-fire mode, a round is inserted into the muzzle, warhead up, fin assembly down, and with the elevation attitude of the barrel it slides down into the "breech." On reaching the breech, the primer at the base of the round strikes a firing pin and the impact sets off the primer that, in turn, explodes the ignition cartridge. The blast from the exploding ignition cartridge ignites the propellants in the round, and the pressure of the gas produced by the burning propellants drives the round out of the barrel. A safety device in the round prevents the detonating fuse from becoming "armed" before it leaves the barrel; and when the round leaves the mortar, it carries the expended primer and ignition cartridge with it. The recoil forces of the round leaving the mortar barrel are transmitted down to the base plate, where they are completely absorbed by the ground.

In the lever-fire mode the round is dropped into the barrel and sits in the breech until the firing pin is operated by the lever or trigger.

The 60-mm mortar uses ammunition that has a "fixed" charge and has a maximum range of about 3,800 yards.

The older M-29A1 81-mm mortar, which is being replaced by the 60-mm mortar, uses ammunition that is called "semifixed" because propellant charges can be added to the rounds to give increased range. The maximum range of the 81-mm mortar, with a standard high-explosive round, is about 5,000 yards.

MINES

M-18A1 Antipersonnel Mine

More commonly called a Claymore Mine, this weapon is a directional, fixed fragmentation mine that is pointed in the direction of an advancing enemy and is either electrically or mechanically fired at an appropriate moment. However, it can be set up as a booby trap above ground, or it can be used in the manner of a conventional land mine, in which case it is detonated "accidentally" by the enemy.

When detonated, the Claymore releases some 700 steel balls, plus its fragmented case, toward the oncoming enemy. It is extremely effective as a defensive weapon for a fixed position that is likely to be subjected to a mass attack by enemy soldiers. The mine comes complete with firing devices and test equipment in a double-pocket bandoleer and weighs about 4 pounds. Because of its versatility and effectiveness, and the fact that it is easy to transport, it is quite popular with the weight-conscious airborne soldier.

TOWED ARTILLERY

M-102 Light Howitzer

The M-102 has been used by the 82nd Airborne and 101st Air Mobile/Air Assault Divisions as an air-dropped field-artillery piece for several years. It has a maximum range, with an armor-piercing shell, of some 16,000 yards. Although it is an effective weapon, it is currently scheduled to be replaced with the larger M-198 15-mm howitzer, which has a range of about 32,000 yards.

ANTITANK WEAPONS

M-72A1/M-72A2 Light Assault Antitank Weapon (LAAW)

The LAAW, as it is more commonly called, is the modern version of the "bazooka." It is supplied to the soldier as a complete unit with the 66-mm rocket already installed in a disposable launch tube. It weighs only 5½ pounds, and although it was designed primarily as an antitank weapon, it is extremely useful against vehicles, pillboxes, gun emplacements, supply dumps, armored command posts, and numerous other types of fortified positions.

It has a maximum range of about 1,000 yards, but its most effective range is around 200 yards. It requires a certain amount of marksmanship to be totally effective. The warhead on the 2¼-pound 66-mm rocket is of the HEAT (High Explosive Anti-Tank) variety, and although it will not pierce the heavy armor on a modern tank, it can certainly stop a tank and inflict considerable damage when used by a skilled operator.

M-47 Dragon

The Dragon is a medium-range (up to about ½ mile), man-portable, shoulder-launched antitank weapon. It is a TOW (Tube-launched, Optically guided, Wire-controlled) weapon that is easy to aim and operate. When the missile is fired, it trails a control wire behind it, through which target information is continually relayed from the optical/electronic sights until either the warhead detonates or the wire is broken as a result of a missed target.

It is a highly accurate weapon with excellent "first round" kill probability—as long as the gunner holds the target in his sights until the missile is seen to impact.

The missile, which comes complete in its own launch tube, weighs some 24 pounds and is 45½ inches long. It is capable of penetrating all known presentday armor.

TOW, BGM-71

Tripod or vehicle-mounted antitank weapon. (Description of this weapon is the same as the helicopter-mounted TOW, which appears later in this chapter.)

MAN-PORTABLE ANTIAIRCRAFT MISSILES

Redeye

The Redeye is shoulder-launched in much the same

manner that an infantryman fires his rifle. The missile consists of two parts, the missile and the launcher. The missile is sealed in its launch tube and cannot be removed in the field except by firing. It is attached to the shoulder launcher and is aimed with an optical-type sight. It weighs approximately 18 pounds, is 4 feet long and 2½ inches in diameter, and is propelled by a solid-fuel rocket motor to a range of about 2 miles. It has a high-explosive warhead that explodes on impact, and the weapon requires a certain degree of skill to be accurate in operation.

Stinger

The Stinger is the most modern "man portable" missile and it is ultimately intended to replace the Redeye. It has an infrared guidance system and the launcher has an IFF (Identification-Friend-or-Foe) system that warns the operator if he is aiming at one of his own aircraft. Like the Redeye, the Stinger missile round is supplied in its own disposable launch tube and requires no field-testing prior to firing, and it can be loaded, aimed, and fired within seconds of a threat arising. The Stinger is some 6 feet long, 2¾ inches in diameter, and weighs 22 pounds. It is propelled by a solid-fuel rocket motor, has a high-explosive contact warhead, and has a range of some 3 miles at supersonic speeds.

HELICOPTERS

UH-1N Huey

The venerable Huey is considered the most widely used helicopter in the world, with more than 9,500 produced from 1950 to the present time. The most modern variant is the UH-1N. It is a twin-engine helicopter manufactured by Bell Helicopter Textron and has a maximum speed of about 130 knots. A combat crew consists of a pilot, copilot, crew chief, and gunner. Its stated mission is to provide utility combat helicopter support to the airborne units in all areas of operation. More often referred to as the "Slick" (when not armed), or just simply the Huey, it is used as a general transporter to carry cargo, either inside or underslung, and it is used extensively as a troop transporter to carry between six and twelve combat troops, depending on how they are equipped and armed.

It can also be used as a primary medical evacuation aircraft and in this configuration there is room for six litter patients and one medical attendant.

As a gunship (it was actually the forerunner of the modern AH-1 and AH-64 gunships), it can be equipped with the 7.62-mm M-60 machine gun, the awesome 7.62-mm GAU-2 B/A minigun, or the 50-caliber M-2 machine gun. It can also be equipped to carry 2.75-inch rocket pods.

CH-47D Chinook

The CH-47D is the current model of the CH-47 series and it is the largest general transport helicopter in use with airborne/air mobile units of the United States Army. Its primary mission is to provide transportation for personnel, and its secondary mission is to transport equipment and supplies and to provide search and rescue services. It is a fully instrumented, all-weather, twin-engine tandem-rotor helicopter built by the Boeing Vertol Company. Capable of carrying up to forty fully armed and equipped combat troops, the

Chinook has a large rear landing ramp for rapid loading and unloading of cargo and vehicles, and it is also equipped to carry underslung loads. As a medical evacuation aircraft it can carry twenty-four litter patients and two medical attendants and for self-protection, it can be armed with two 7.62-mm M-60 machine guns or two .50-caliber M-2 machine guns. During the Vietnam era several Chinooks were also armed with grenade launchers and numerous minigun pods for special operations.

In combat the normal Chinook crew consists of a pilot, copilot, crew chief, and gunner.

The Chinook has a maximum speed of 190 miles per hour, and the most modern versions have a sealed fuselage that permits them to float without the use of external flotation devices in the event of a forced landing on water.

AH-1 Cobra

The Cobra, manufactured by the Bell Textron Corporation, is a fast attack helicopter currently in service with the airborne units in several variants, such as the AH-1J and AH-1T. More commonly referred to as the "Snake," the Cobra's mission is that of armed escort and fire support. It carries a crew of two, pilot and gunner, with the gunner sitting in front of the pilot, and can be armed with a variety of weaponry from 2.75-inch rocket packs, 7.62-mm minigun pods, 20-mm cannons, 40-mm grenade launchers, and both self-guided and TOW missiles. (TOW is a derivative of Tube-launched, Optically guided, Wire-controlled guided missile.)

AH-64 Apache

The most modern of attack helicopters, the AH-64

entered service with the Army in 1984 and is considered the ugliest-looking helicopter in the world. However, it is also the most potent attack helicopter of all time, as it is equipped with some highly sophisticated weapons systems such as day/night forward-looking infrared, laser ranger/designator, and laser tracker, and can deliver tremendous fire power under most battlefield conditions.

It can carry up to seventy-six 2.75-inch rockets or sixteen Hellfire antitank missiles, or a mixture of both, and it is also armed with a single 30-mm cannon.

UH-60 Black Hawk

The Black Hawk is the Army's most modern combat assault transport helicopter and it is ultimately intended to replace the UH-1N Huey. It can carry eleven fully equipped troops, or four litters with one medical attendant. It is manufactured from the most modern materials available, titanium, Kevlar (R), glass fiber, and Nomex Honeycomb (R). The Black Hawk has a maximum speed of about 180 miles per hour and can be armed with two M-60 door-mounted guns.

The 101st Airborne started to take delivery of the Black Hawk in 1979 and the 82nd Airborne started to take delivery in 1981.

HELICOPTER ANTITANK AND SELF-DEFENSE MISSILES

TOW Missile

The word TOW, as stated previously, means Tube-launched, Optically guided, Wire-controlled, and it is an antitank missile system that is carried by attack helicopters (although it can be used as a ground-based system mounted on small vehicles).

The TOW missile system, both in the air and on the ground, is considered the finest antitank weapon in the world because of its accuracy and destructive power at long ranges. When the weapon is fired, the helicopter is usually at a hover or moving at a slow speed. The missile leaves its storage tube trailing a long electrical wire through which the helicopter pilot/gunner actually steers the missile to the target with the use of an optical sighting device. As the gunner holds the target in his sights, electronic signals are fed to the missile to control its flight. Once the missile impacts, the wire will automatically be cut from the launching tube on the helicopter and the pilot will be free to move his craft out of the area.

The missile weighs some 43 pounds and is 3 feet 9 inches long and 6 inches in diameter. It is propelled by a solid-fuel rocket motor and a solid-fuel booster unit, and has a range of approximately 2.6 miles.

Air-to-Air Stinger

This is basically the same missile as the shoulder-launched weapon mentioned earlier, but modified to be carried by a helicopter as an air-to-air self-defense weapon. It is presently being tested and has been accepted for use on attack helicopters.

4
Historical Development

It is a little-known fact that since the inception of airborne/air mobile forces, shortly after World War I, only thirty-seven major airborne assaults have been conducted under actual combat conditions by all the armies in the world combined. The most recent of these assaults was carried out by the U.S. Ranger Battalions and the 82nd Airborne Division during the rescue of American and other students from the island of Grenada.

Despite the many successes of American airborne operations during World War II, Korea, and Vietnam, the United States was the last of the major nations to accept totally the concept of airborne operations as a useful method of rapidly deploying troops and equipment. Yet, the concept of using airborne troops was first seriously considered by two individual Americans who were generations apart.

The first was the great politician-ambassador-philosopher-scientist Benjamin Franklin. In 1784, the year after Franklin had witnessed the first man-carrying balloon flight in France, he wrote: "And where is the prince who could so afford to cover his country with troops for its defense, as that ten thousand men descending from the clouds might not, in many places, cause an infinite deal of mischief before a force could be brought together to repel them."

The second individual, William "Billy" Mitchell, was one of the most far-sighted of all American military men. He made Franklin's dream become a reality some 123 years later. On October 17, 1918, Mitchell, then a colonel with the Army Air Corps, was in charge of the Aviation Forces attached to General Jack Pershing's American Expeditionary Forces in Europe. Pershing was trying to drive his army up through the Argonne Forest and it was being plagued with attacks from German aircraft. Mitchell had presented an innovative plan to send his aircraft on bombing missions far behind the German lines in order to disrupt the enemy's supply and communications system. However, Pershing told his colonel that he was not interested in the plan. Instead, Pershing asked Mitchell to organize his air force to stop the German air attacks over the American front lines and gain complete control of the air in the entire American sector. Once this was accomplished, Pershing wanted Mitchell to send his aircraft over the German lines to attack the massed infantry and artillery that were threatening the American forces. Pershing further informed Mitchell that if there was any time left, the air force should gather information on enemy movements along the entire front line.

Mitchell readily agreed to comply with Pershing's request. In fact, unknown to Pershing, Mitchell had already organized his forces to do exactly what the general was planning. Mitchell went on to inform Pershing that he had a plan to assist the American forces in an assault that was still in the planning stages. Pershing's staff had been organizing a final, major thrust against the Germans that was to commence in the spring of 1919. The Allied Forces, led by the Americans, were to drive up toward the heart of Germany. Pershing felt that the Germans would immediately surrender if such an assault succeeded.

The first target was the city of Metz, into which the Germans were pouring reinforcements. They suspected that the Allied Forces would attempt to take it within the near future. When Mitchell informed Pershing that he would have some twelve hundred bombers available to him by the spring of 1919, and that he could put ten fully equipped infantrymen equipped with parachutes in each aircraft and drop them into Metz, the general immediately began to listen.

Mitchell quickly explained that he would like to use the troops of the 1st Division. He thought he could get some twelve thousand of them into Metz within a matter of hours. Pershing was awed with the possibility. He knew that if only one-tenth of that number were landed in the Metz area, the force would cause havoc among the Germans. Metz could certainly be taken in a very short period of time and with few casualties.

Pershing doubted that such an assault could be put into operation. But he knew that if it were possible, his brilliant aviation officer could do it. Mitchell was surprised when Pershing approved the idea and ordered him to work out a detailed plan, but Pershing also cautioned Mitchell that the plan should not interfere with the orders he had just given.

Elated at the general's response, Mitchell immediately instructed his operations officer, Major Lewis Brereton, to start working out the details. It was a massive task. And before Brereton began solving the problems, the war came to a halt.

As a matter of record, air-dropping soldiers behind the enemy lines was not conceived by Mitchell. In fact, the French had been doing it throughout the war with two-man saboteur teams. However, Billy Mitchell was among the first to conceive the idea of a massed drop of fighting men. There is little doubt that if the drop had been accomplished at Metz, it would have been successful.

When World War I ended, Mitchell tried to persuade the Chiefs of Staff to pursue the idea of massed troop drops and he arranged a demonstration which was held at Kelly Field, San Antonio, Texas. A Martin MB-2 bomber flew over the field and six soldiers parachuted to the ground. Two minutes and fifty seconds after they jumped from the aircraft, the six soldiers landed in a designated target area, assembled two machine guns, and began firing into a simulated "enemy" position.

The various generals assigned to evaluate the demonstration were not impressed. They dismissed the whole idea as ridiculous. However, they did agree that the parachute was useful to the military and that more development work was required. As a result, the Army Air Corps commenced a program at Wright Field to further develop the parachute. The emphasis was almost all technical, concentrating on the development of a safe and reliable chute. No authorization was given for the development of a plan to drop large numbers of soldiers into battle.

Since the Army Chiefs were not interested in parachuting troops into battle, Mitchell took another tack. He tried to persuade the Army Chiefs to look at the transportation of large numbers of infantry and their supporting equipment by transport aircraft and gliders (now termed *air-land operations*). The Chiefs of Staff were not quite as negative about air-land proposals, but they were reluctant to commit themselves to major development.

In Europe, however, the thinking was almost the opposite. The British, Germans, Italians, French, and Russians saw air-drop and air-land operations as a vital dimension of modern warfare and they began to experiment with the concept.

The Germans, who were prohibited from training pilots in powered aircraft under the terms of the World War I Armistice, started to train pilots in gliders. During the late 1920s and early 1930s, government-operated schools trained thousands of pilots within a short period of time. By 1932 Germany had an estimated sixty thousand qualified civilian glider pilots, and it was from this pool of qualified aviators that the Luftwaffe was rapidly developed within the few years prior to World War II.

Although sport parachuting by civilians and troop-drop techniques by the Army were subject to experimental development, the Armed Forces put far more emphasis on glider training. In 1936 the German Army formed its first parachute regiment and started to train its troops. Within a short time, valuable lessons concerning massed troop drops were learned by the German military leaders. They were later put to good use, particularly in the opening rounds of World War II.

The Chiefs of Staff of the Italian Air Force, led by General Giulio Douhet, were more adventurous than most military men. They worked hard at developing massed troop-drop techniques and also the resupply of troops by parachute. Between 1927 and 1931 Italian paratroopers trained extensively. Airborne exercises, simulated combat drops, and air-land operations were regular features of Italian military life. By 1930 several major operations were conducted in North Africa. Hundreds of troops were dropped in a single assault from tight formations of lumbering transport aircraft.

The British and French developed their air-drop and air-land techniques at a more leisurely pace during the late 1920s and early 1930s. The British eventually accelerated their programs as a result of information that was coming out of the Soviet Union.

The Russians, putting it bluntly, went "hog wild" with parachuting, both civilian and military, and made the combined efforts of all other nations look trivial by comparison. A national parachute club, the Osoaviakhim, trained individual parachutists at an incredible rate and by 1932 the Soviets were claiming that they had over half a million trained civilian parachutists. By 1934 that figure was in excess of one million.

As thousands of Russian civilians were leaping from aircraft, balloons, towers, and tall buildings with parachutes strapped to their backs, the Soviet Army began to consider using the parachute for massed troop deployments. However, during the early days of the Russian "leaping Lemming-like syndrome," civilian casualties caused by parachute failures were incredibly high. This did not seem to deter the growth of the sport, perhaps because parachute jumping was considered a highly patriotic sport. Although it was not exactly an official civic requirement, jumping was so "fashionable" that it became almost mandatory for any full-blooded Soviet citizen, male or female.

Although official figures were never published, it is known that several hundred Soviet citizens died as a result of parachute failures in the late 1920s. Far from deterring newcomers, the fatalities probably enhanced the glamour value of the sport among the bored Soviet populace. But the military leaders became concerned at the prospect of hundreds of soldiers plummeting to their deaths because of failed parachutes. The Soviet military leaders reasoned that they could tolerate about four or five deaths per one hundred men in a single jump, but not much more. It appears that parachute manufacturers in the Soviet Union at that time could not guarantee a lower failure rate. As a result, the military leaders promptly dispatched one of their most experienced parachutists, Leonid Minov, on a world tour to study the technical developments of other nations. If possible, he was to bring back a reliable parachute that was already being manufactured.

Minov's tour concluded with the selection of the American Irving parachute. He returned to Russia with one of every model that Irving manufactured at that time. Shortly after his return, Minov was ordered to establish the Soviet Army's first parachute regiment, and the Soviet military leaders guaranteed that he would have no difficulty obtaining volunteers.

The Soviet Union held its first major air show in Moscow on August 18, 1933. It was intended primarily to show other nations that the Soviets were ahead in what was being termed in military circles the "air supremacy race." On that day, two large bombers trundled over the showgrounds and forty-six fully armed soldiers parachuted down in front of about ten thousand Soviets and a score of invited foreign observers.

The foreign observers, mostly military, were surprised at the number of parachutists, and the event was hailed as the world record for a massed drop. However, a greater surprise awaited these observers: another large transport rumbled overhead and a small tank floated down on a large parachute. (The total effect of this stunt was marred somewhat by the fact that the tank could not be started when it landed and had to be pushed off the showgrounds.)

In 1935 the Soviets held a similar show, dropping eight hundred fully armed troops onto the showgrounds. Within minutes these troops had set up a "defensive perimeter" and almost immediately several eighteen-man gliders appeared and landed to deploy further troops. The gliders were then moved quickly to one side to make way for eight large transport aircraft, which landed in a short distance. Each disgorged a cargo of two howitzers, which began firing blanks.

Military observers were amazed, particularly the British and German attachés. Respective governments were soon informed about the Soviet developments.

In 1936, as the German and the British started to accelerate their parachute training, the Soviets held two air shows. The first was at Minsk, where the Soviets air-dropped some twelve hundred troops as well as air-landing tanks and artillery. The invited foreign military observers were again surprised. But when they attended the second air show near Moscow, some two weeks later, several of the observers, notably the British, German, and American, became acutely alarmed.

The Soviets proudly displayed their aerial achievements again. As a finale they parachuted some five thousand combat troops onto the showgrounds in a simulated assault. The last of the parachutists had barely landed when gliders and powered transport aircraft arrived and air-landed small tanks, vehicles, horses, and artillery.

The result of the demonstration caused the German military leaders to further intensify their efforts in air-mobile warfare, while the British increased their efforts more modestly. The Italians felt that they were as advanced as the Soviets, which indeed they were, and they simply continued with their established programs. In America the news was met by big yawns on the part of all the senior military leaders. Nothing further was done.

Although no progress was made in America in the use of paratroopers, some progress with the air-land concept was being realized. The Army Chiefs had realized that air-landing was a useful method of rapidly transporting troops and battlefield supplies over long distances. In 1931, in a demonstration of "hemispheric defense" the Army airlifted an artillery battery and its equipment into Panama as part of an exercise. In 1933 they conducted a similar exercise with a full artillery battalion, and in that same year an astute Army Air Corps officer, Captain George Kenney, air-landed a small infantry detachment behind "enemy" lines during a major exercise in Delaware. The consternation and confusion he caused, by the tactical advantage the infantry detachment achieved, created further interest in the entire air-mobile concept. However, development still moved forward at a slow pace.

On April 9, 1940, the Germans attacked Norway and Denmark using paratroopers and air-landed infantry as spearhead units. Norwegian and Danish defenders were taken almost completely by surprise, and within a matter of a few days the Germans had suppressed the small Danish Army and gained a firm foothold in Norway. The Germans eventually gained control of Norway, despite fierce resistance by the Norwegians and their British allies.

Such a decisive use of air-drop (parachuting) and air-landed (landing and disembarking troops) troops finally jolted the American military strategists into realizing that they had almost "missed the boat" by not paying more attention to the tremendous potential of airborne forces. What surprised almost everyone—British, French, Soviets, and Americans—was the speed and daring with which the German assault was carried out. It was obvious that Norway would not have fallen so easily if more-traditional assault methods had been employed.

The Chiefs of Staff, under considerable pressure from questioning government officials, newspaper reporters, and the public in general, ordered studies to be conducted immediately to determine how the United States could quickly develop an air capability to equal the Germans'. When the call went out for "Air Infantry" studies to be conducted, almost every branch of the Armed Forces immediately entered competition with one another. The Navy and the Marine Corps lost out quickly. Most of the competition ended up within the Army, specifically between the Army Air Corps and the Infantry. Each group felt that they should have control of the new "soon to be established" force and the Air Corps proposed such names as "Air Grenadiers" and "Marines of the Air Corps."

The Chiefs of Staff considered all proposals and accepted the recommendations of Major William Lee, who was attached to the staff of the Chief of Infantry. On June 25, 1940, the Commandant of the Infantry School, Brigadier General Asa Singleton, was directed to organize, as quickly as possible, a parachute test platoon of volunteers from the 29th Infantry Regiment stationed at Fort Benning, Georgia. Shortly afterward, the Commanding General of the 2nd Infantry Division was ordered to begin detailed studies of the requirements and procedures necessary for the deployment and use of "air-transported" troops.

When officer volunteers were requested from the 29th Infantry, Lieutenant William Ryder was the first to step forward. He became the platoon leader, with Lieutenant James Bassett assigned as assistant platoon leader. More than two hundred enlisted men volunteered for the new platoon. Ryder and Bassett selected forty-eight on the basis of high standards of health, good service records, and rugged physical characteristics.

Ryder moved his platoon into a tent camp at Lawson Field, the Fort Benning Airfield, and secured an empty hangar where the platoon organized for training and for packing parachutes. As Ryder and Bassett tried to work out details of the training program, they were assisted by William Lee, now a lieutenant colonel, and who was later to earn for himself the unofficial title "Father of the Airborne."

Lee was a strong advocate of the airborne concept long before the Chiefs of Staff were mesmerized by the German assault on Norway. It was his recommendation that had been accepted concerning the formation of the test platoon. He was intent on seeing that the new platoon received all the help it could get.

He personally recommended to the Chief of Infantry that in order to train the platoon in the shortest possible time, the entire unit should be moved to Hightstown, New Jersey, for a week's special training on the giant parachute-drop towers that had been manufactured for the New York World's Fair. The towers were owned by the Safe Parachute Company. Lee had persuaded the company that their use by an Army test team was in the nation's best interest.

The company readily agreed. Some eighteen days after the formation of the platoon, the entire unit was in New Jersey. Assistance from the staff of the Safe Parachute Company was readily provided, and within a few days the platoon was operating from the 250-foot-high towers during every minute of daylight. Soon the troops were operating from them in near darkness; and finally in almost total darkness.

Dropping from the towers not only gave a very realistic touch to parachute training, it helped build morale. The soldiers learned that their parachutes would function correctly when they were properly packed and used in the correct manner. Senior members of the Army who visited the platoon during training could see for themselves that the towers provided realistic preparation for actual drops. After their visits, senior officers unanimously recommended to the Chief of Staff of the Army that the Army acquire its own towers. Shortly afterward, the Chief of Staff accepted these recommendations and ordered two towers to be erected at Fort Benning. Some time later, two more towers were ordered and installed at Fort Benning. (Three of the original towers are still standing today.)

On the morning of August 16, 1940, shortly after their return from training on the towers in New Jersey, the test platoon prepared for its first jump from an aircraft. The men boarded a Douglas B-18 bomber, a variant of the DC-2 civilian airliner, which had been slightly modified to carry paratroopers, and took off from Lawson Field for the first official parachute drop by the United States Army.

This was not a massed drop. Lieutenant Ryder was to be the first man to jump, and if everything went well, the next man would follow, and so on until the aircraft was empty. Ryder realized that his men were wondering whom he would assign to follow him. Before he could make his decision, the enlisted men requested that he allow them to draw lots for the privilege. Ryder readily agreed.

The lottery was won by Private William King. When the B-18 came back over Lawson Field, Ryder jumped out the door and his parachute deployed properly. King was then ordered to jump. As he leaped out the door of the aircraft, he became the first enlisted soldier to make an official parachute jump as a member of the United States Army.

Individual jumping practice from the B-18 continued for more than a week until the entire platoon had at least five jumps each. Then, on August 29, 1940, the platoon made the first massed military parachute jump in the United States in front of some of the most high-ranking officers in the Army. As a result of the success of this jump, the Army issued orders for the immediate formation of parachute combat units of battalion size.

The first such unit was built around the test platoon and was designed as the 501st Parachute Battalion. Its commanding officer was Major William Miley, who, within a year, rose to the rank of major general and commanded the 17th Airborne Division.

To accelerate the training of the 501st and prepare the formation of further parachute battalions, Army engineers, in conjunction with the Civilian Conservation Corps, cleared several large tree- and shrub-covered areas in the vicinity of Fort Benning. Three large training buildings were erected along with additional administrative offices, living quarters, and the new 250-foot-high jump towers.

Aircraft were needed. On instructions from General "Hap" Arnold, head of Army Aviation, the Air Corps assigned a new group to Lawson Field to support the training of paratroopers. Hap Arnold also assigned several Douglas B-18s and various other aircraft to the parachute unit.

Private Aubrey Eberhart, one of the first members of the 501st Parachute Battalion, was tormented by some of his friends because of his acute nervousness prior to jumping out of an aircraft. When his friends suggested that he did not have full control of his faculties, he decided to prove them wrong. He leaped out the door of the aircraft and screamed one word that was heard by everyone, both in the aircraft, in the air, and on the ground. That word, "Geronimo," caused so much hilarity that it was adopted as the battle cry of the 501st and has been used extensively by paratroopers ever since.

On July 1, 1941, a second battalion was activated and was designated the 502nd. Men from the 501st were assigned to establish the 502nd, but as the new battalion was far beneath the required strength, Lieutenant Colonel Lee began recruiting volunteers from the 9th Infantry Division stationed at Fort Bragg, North Carolina. The initial response was overwhelming. Four hundred enlisted men, many of them sergeants and warrant officers, proved quite prepared to "take a bust" and drop their rank in order to be accepted for parachute training. Lee had little difficulty in bringing the 502nd up to strength.

The formation of the 501st and 502nd Parachute Battalions led to the formation of many others, including the famous, all-black, 555th Parachute Battalion, which was created in December 1943.

As the paratrooper battalions grew toward division size, advances were being made in other forms of airborne warfare. The 2nd Infantry Division, in conjunction with the Army Air Corps, started experimenting with troop transporation and air-land techniques. The Air Corps formed specialized transport groups for landing combat-ready troops.

On October 10, 1941, the Army's first Glider Infantry Battalion was activated. It was officially designated the 88th Glider Infantry Battalion and was placed under the command of Lieutenant Colonel Elbridge Chapman, Jr. (Chapman later rose to the rank of major general and commanded the 13th Airborne Division.)

By 1942 William Lee, a full colonel, was accepted as the foremost authority in the development of parachute units. He recommended to General Lesley McNair, Commander of United States Army Ground Forces, that two full Airborne Divisions be established. McNair agreed immediately.

On August 15, 1942, at Camp Claiborne, Louisiana, the first two Airborne Divisions were created. For the first, the name of the 82nd Motorized Infantry Division was changed to the 82nd Airborne Division. The second was created by disbanding the reserve 101st Infantry Division and reactivating it as a regular unit at Camp Claiborne under the name of the 101st Airborne Division. Initially, personnel and equipment for both Airborne Divisions were supplied by dividing the now-deactivated 82nd Motorized Infantry Division into two groups.

In the same year, the small parachute-training unit that had been established at Lawson Field was further expanded and officially named the Parachute School. Since then it has seen a succession of name changes, ranging from the "Airborne School" in 1946 to "Airborne Army Aviation Group," "Airborne Department," "Airborn-air Mobility Department," and finally, as of 1982, the "4th Airborne Training Battalion, The School Brigade."

World War II saw the creation of various other Airborne Divisions, all of which have since been deactivated. Only two divisions, the 82nd and 101st, remain, although there are plans to create a third Airborne within the very near future (probably by the time this book is in print).

The official titles of the two remaining divisions are

82nd Airborne Division and 101st Airborne Division (Air Assault). The roles of the two divisions differ somewhat. A simple explanation is that the 82nd is more of a paratrooper division, whereas the 101st is more of an air-land division (although in the 101st, parachuting is still a prime requirement and is frequently used).

In terms of battlefield equipment, the 101st is almost self-sufficient, having its own attack and transport helicopters and various other aircraft, whereas the 82nd has a limited number of transport helicopters and relies on other forces for almost all its air support.

Although female personnel have always played a major role in the Airborne organizations, that role has, by Congressional decree, excluded the use of combat arms. Parachute training was always considered a pure combat-arms skill; therefore, females have never been required to undergo such training. However, there exists a very sensible rule in the United States military that parachute packers, known as "riggers," must be qualified parachutists and must maintain their proficiency on an annual basis.

In the early 1970s there was an acute shortage of riggers. The Department of the Army, realizing that other nations had always used female personnel as riggers, authorized a modified parachute-training course in order to "qualify" females for the job. As a result, on December 14, 1973, the first two women, Private Johnson and Private Kutsch, were graduated from the Airborne School by making their first parachute jump from an aircraft. Since that time, females have enrolled in the parachute course on a regular basis and they play a vital role in the modern Army.

Finally, although several types of Airborne insignia have been used by both glider and parachute units since 1942, an official insignia was not authorized until 1949. According to the official description, "the insignia will consist of a white parachute and glider on a blue disc, approximately two and one-quarter inches in diameter, with a red border. . . ." Today, the sign of an Airborne-qualified soldier is a parachute set on eagles' wings. Although it is a simple badge, it represents a strong tradition.

Army Airborne has served this nation well, from the battlefields of World War II in Europe and the Pacific, through Korea, Vietnam, and most recently Grenada. Their battlefield conduct has more than earned them the honor of being called one of the world's fighting elite, and their esprit de corps is still one of the highest among military groups.

5

BATTLEFIELD LOG:
Wilhelmina Canal Bridge, Best, Holland, 1944

At 1000 hours on Sunday, September 17, 1944 an armada of fighter aircraft, fighter bombers, and transport aircraft, some towing gliders, set out from England and headed for Holland. This was Operation Market, the airborne phase of Operation Market-Garden; Operation Garden was the ground phase and would commence when the soldiers in the transport aircraft parachuted into Holland.

The aircraft, gliders, and paratroopers were all members of the newly formed First Allied Airborne Army, which was comprised of squadrons of American and British troop-carrying aircraft and gliders; the American 101st Airborne Division; the 82nd Airborne Division and the 17th Airborne Division; three British Airborne Divisions; and the 1st Polish Parachute Brigade.

The mission of this conglomerate of airborne assault troops was to open a sixty-mile "corridor" along a narrow road that ran almost due north and south through the heart of German-occupied Holland. Once the corridor was established, XXX Corps (called Thirty Corps) of the British Army, led by the armored units of the Irish Guards, would attempt to drive as rapidly as possible from the Dutch/Belgian border in the south to the town of Arnhem on the river Rhine in the north.

The narrow road that was the center of the "corridor" was vital to the entire operation, as the majority of the terrain in the lowlands of Holland was flat and boggy, making it impossible for tanks and mechanized vehicles to cross it. Another feature of Holland is that it is crisscrossed with rivers and canals; therefore, it has a profusion of bridges. The narrow road that the airborne troops were attempting to keep open was no exception. On average there was at least one bridge every four or five miles.

Intelligence information indicated that the Germans planned to destroy all the major bridges along the road if the Allied Forces started to advance through Holland. This would seriously hamper the advance of armor and supporting infantry. The Allied Commanders hoped they could prevent the destruction of most of the bridges by the rapid deployment of the airborne forces, whose primary function was to seize and hold the bridges.

Once the bridges were taken, the airborne commanders were then to assign as many troops as possible to the task of keeping the enemy away from the road in order for British armored units to advance.

The sixty-mile stretch of road was divided into three sections for the airborne assault. The northern section around Arnhem was the responsibility of the British paratroopers; the midsection, from the town of Nijmegen south toward the town of Uden, was the responsibility of the 82nd Airborne Division; and the southern section, a sixteen-mile stretch of the road from the town of

Veghel down to Eindhoven, was the responsibility of the 101st Airborne.

The ten-mile stretch of road south of Eindhoven to the Allied front line was to be taken by the advancing British armored units, who were scheduled to move out from the Dutch/Belgian border some thirty minutes after the airborne troops were dropped. The first of the British armored units, the Irish Guards, were scheduled to link up with the 101st Airborne on the outskirts of Eindhoven at 2000 hours the same evening; from there they were allowed some forty hours to get to Arnhem.

The entire Market-Garden operation was intended to give the Allies a direct road through to Germany and the Plain of Westphalia, where Allied armor could operate easily. A secondary benefit was that the German forces to the west of the road would be cut off from Germany and surrounded. After that, they would have to fight with their backs to the North Sea.

The 101st dropped into their assigned areas on time and in good order. On the first day they quickly seized the bridges at Veghel and St. Oedenrode, but the bridges at the town of Zon were destroyed by the Germans before they could be taken. Heavy German resistance prevented an advance south to Eindhoven on the first day for the link-up with the advancing British armor, but it did not matter, as the British had also encountered stiff resistance and did not reach Eindhoven that evening.

Shortly after the landing, H Company, 3rd Battalion, 502nd Regiment, was sent to take the town of Best, about four miles to the west of Zon. This was simply a precautionary maneuver, designed to give flank protection to the rest of the regiment. (Intelligence reports indicated that Best was "lightly held.") Best was situated some six miles northwest of Eindhoven between a narrow road and a set of railroad tracks that led to the town of Boxtel. About one mile south of Best, both road and railroad crossed the Wilhelmina Canal. Initially, these bridges were not of any real interest to the 101st.

However, when the main Zon bridge was destroyed, the bridges south of Best became critically important, as they could be used by the British to bypass Zon. Captain Robert Jones, who was leading H company to take Best, knew nothing of the problems concerning the loss of the bridge at Zon. He had problems of his own, as he was experiencing terrible difficulties in his attempts to take the supposedly "lightly held" town. The area around Best was in fact being occupied by almost one thousand men of the German 59th Infantry Division and its supporting artillery units. H Company came under heavy fire from well-entrenched troops as they neared the town.

Jones managed to get the company as far as the main crossroads of the town but he was starting to take heavy casualties. He had just launched an attempt to push the enemy back from the crossroads when he received a message from his battalion commander, Colonel Robert Cole. Cole ordered Jones to send his Engineer Platoon, his 2nd Platoon, and his light machine-gun units down to take the bridges on the Wilhelmina Canal. Realizing that he could not hold his ground near the crossroads if he sent these units to the bridges, Jones pulled back into the surrounding pine woods and set up a defensive position.

This done, he ordered Lieutenant Edward Wierzbowski to take the 2nd Platoon and the Engineer Platoon south and seize the canal bridges. The lieutenant set off with a greatly depleted force. He had already lost twelve men from the 2nd Platoon in the skirmish at the crossroads, and he was without his machine-gun section and his platoon leader. The accompanying Engineer Platoon was in no better shape than the 2nd Platoon, as it too had taken casualties during the foray with the enemy and was missing an entire squad.

Wierzbowski sent his lead scout, Private First Class Joe Mann, to find a clear path through the woods while the rest of the group set out after him. It was almost sunset when the combined platoons left the remainder of the company. The lieutenant urged them to move as quickly as possible as he wanted to arrive at the bridges before dark. However, the platoons had moved only a short distance when Mann came back to report that a considerable number of enemy were hidden in the woods. The Germans had cleared fire lanes through the pine trees. Machine guns were set up along the lanes and the enemy had a clear field of fire if any attempt was made to cross the lanes.

When the lieutenant tried crossing the first lane, enemy machine guns opened up immediately. It became obvious that the Germans had set up a fairly good defensive system. Wierzbowski pulled his men back from the fire lane, unprepared to risk losing any more of his men in an attempt to get to the bridges before dark. He then sent Mann off in an easterly direction to find a better track.

Joe Mann, an excellent scout, quickly discovered that the entire woods were laced with the death-trap fire lanes. Maneuvering carefully, he pinpointed areas where the lanes narrowed and enemy machine guns were less favorably positioned. He informed the lieutenant that the platoons could cross the lanes in quick bursts without suffering any casualties. Wierzbowski agreed to try.

Mann was right. As the troops continued through the

forest, they chose the crossing points Mann had selected on the lanes and no losses were incurred.

It was dark and raining when the patrol reached the
edge of the woods. Joe Mann was quite happy about
the weather conditions, since the noise of the rain made
his scouting task easier. An open field now lay in front
of them. Mann set out to crawl across. A few minutes
later, he returned and signaled Wierzbowski to follow.
The patrol moved out. Once across the field, Mann led
his men around a small marshy area and up to the
northern bank of the canal.

Then, very slowly, the men followed the canal bank
toward the bridge until they came to a small dock basin
on the side of the canal. Mann scouted around the
basin, returning a few minutes later to say that the area
behind the basin was crowded with German soldiers. It
would be too risky to lead the entire patrol through that
area.

Just in front of the patrol were two large gantries,
one on either side of the entrance to the basin. A
narrow catwalk was suspended between the gantries,
angling out over the water. Mann judged that if the
men were careful, they could crawl over the catwalk
and continue along the canal bank to the bridge, which
Wierzbowski estimated was about five hundred yards
farther on.

Wierzbowski was prepared to take the chance. He
sent Mann on ahead to scout the area beyond the basin.
If no shooting was heard, and Mann did not return
within a few minutes, Wierzbowski would lead his men
over the dangling, wet, slippery catwalk.

Mann disappeared. After a few minutes of silence,
Wierzbowski determined that his scout had not run into
trouble. With Wierzbowski in the lead, his men started
across the dangerous catwalk.

Once across the catwalk, Wierzbowski led his men along the canal bank for a short distance before meeting his scout coming the other way. Mann informed the lieutenant that he had halted when he heard raised voices from a group of enemy soldiers somewhere in front of him. He had not seen the bridge, but he suspected that the enemy soldiers he had heard were guarding the approach. He had decided to return in order to ensure that the patrol was safely over the crosswalk. Wierzbowski ordered the patrol to set up in a defensive position while he returned with Mann to the point where he had heard the soldiers.

After creeping stealthily forward for some time, Mann signaled that they were at the position where he had heard the enemy. Detecting no sound or movement, they continued forward until they could see the approach to the bridge.

They turned back to meet the remainder of the patrol when, suddenly, a shot rang out. They dived for cover.

In front of them was a German soldier with his rifle pointed in the air. He shouted across toward the far bank of the canal. Someone answered him. The guard then proceeded to patrol the area between the two paratroopers and the remainder of their platoon.

Wierzbowski and Mann watched him carefully. Every few minutes he would fire his rifle in the air and call out to the guard on the other side of the canal to let him know that he was still alive. Then he resumed patrolling in front of the two paratroopers.

Pulling his knife, Mann signaled to the lieutenant that he could easily take the guard. Wierzbowski shook his head, negative. Within a few minutes the soldier on the far bank would realize that something was wrong and raise the alarm. Wierzbowski realized that he and

Mann had managed to reach the bridge just as the enemy were changing their guards. He suspected that they would have to remain in their present position until the next guard change.

Almost half an hour had passed when the sound of shots and exploding grenades came from the direction of the remainder of the patrol. The enemy had discovered Wierzbowski's men and had launched an attack, killing several men. The nearby guard was distracted by the shots. Mann saw his chance and attacked, killing the guard. Then he and the lieutenant scrambled back along the bank toward the remainder of the patrol, amid a hail of rifle, machine gun, and mortar fire.

As they reached the patrol, an 88-mm gun opened up on their position. Wierzbowski ordered his men to fall back some fifty or sixty yards and set up a new defensive position. Mann covered the retreat of the patrol, wiping out a six-man squad of enemy soldiers that attempted to pursue them. When he reached the new position on the canal bank, Wierzbowski informed him that everyone was low on ammunition. Only eighteen men were left. He gave orders that there was to be no unnecessary shooting. Only clearly visible attacking enemy were to be fired upon, regardless of how long they were under attack.

Shortly before midnight, when they had been discovered, it had been raining heavily. By 0300 hours it was still raining, but the Germans had finally stopped shooting. Wierzbowski had no means of contacting Captain Jones and the remainder of the company, except by sending out a messenger. He knew that the only soldier who could get through to the company was Mann, but he would not risk sending a man who was such a valuable soldier in a fire fight. He decided that Captain

Jones would get worried soon enough and send out a patrol to see what was happening.

Captain Jones was indeed worried when he heard nothing from Wierzbowski. The patrols he sent were driven out of the woods by enemy fire. Furthermore, Captain Jones had other problems. The Germans were pressing his position. Jones called for the remainder of the 3rd Battalion to assist as he realized that enemy strength in the Best area had been badly underestimated.

When dawn broke, Wierzbowski and his defenders finally saw the bridge, a little more than a hundred yards from their position. No guards were on the paratroopers' side of the bridge, at least not on the direct approaches. But across the road from the bridge, Wierzbowski saw several gun emplacements covering the approaches. Behind him, in the buildings around the dock basin, he knew a group of the enemy was hidden. On the south side of the canal, near the bridge approaches, he could see a barracks-type building. In front of it he could see several machine guns and 88-mm-gun pits.

Shortly after dawn Mann saw a group of soldiers approaching from the woods to the north. Wierzbowski ordered the men not to fire until the enemy came within close range. At first Wierzbowski interpreted the enemy approach as an attack. But when Mann spotted a number of wounded men among the enemy, Wierzbowski realized that the enemy were retreating from the woods. When the enemy were within fifty yards, their colleagues on the bridge began shouting at them, but it was too late. Wierzbowski gave the order to fire. At least forty enemy soldiers were killed in a hail of deadly accurate fire.

Shortly after 1000 hours two men appeared on the bridge, one an enemy soldier, the second a civilian.

Laden with their equipment, officers and men of the 82nd Airborne Division await takeoff aboard a C-47 for Airborne landings in Holland.

With the words "ready-go" the jumpmaster sends these "Angels" of the famed 11th Airborne Division hurtling into the sky over the fields of Japan.

Men of the 501st and 502nd Battle Groups of the 101st Airborne Division float to earth carrying full combat equipment.

Pilots of Troop B, 3rd Squadron, 17th Cavalry can trace their military historical lineage to General Custer's command at Little Big Horn and are called to action, like their predecessors, by a horn.

Soldiers of the 1st Squadron, 9th Cavalry, 1st Cavalry Division (Airmobile) learn rappelling from a 35-foot tower at Fort Benning, Ga. After five jumps from the tower the men move to helicopters and make three more jumps from a height of 60 feet. After these eight jumps the men are considered qualified "sky troopers."

Pathfinders of the 101st Airborne Divison (Airmobile) guide incoming UH-1D helicopters, which will extract the members of Company C, 1st Battalion (Airborne), 503rd Infantry, during field exercises of the Advanced Infantry Training Course.

U.S. Army and Air Force personnel at Pope Air Force Base,
load an 82nd Airborne Division OH-13 helicopter into an Air
Force Cargo-type C-124 aircraft for transporting.

Soldiers of the
101st Airborne
Brigade in
Vietnam.

Paratroopers of Company B, 2nd Battalion (Airborne), 327th Infantry, combat assualt from UH-ID helicopters.

Wierzbowski ordered his men not to shoot as he was afraid the civilian was an innocent Dutchman. After twenty minutes on the bridge, the two men left and shortly afterward there was a tremendous explosion.

The soldier and the civilian had been on the bridge setting the firing mechanism on the preset demolition charges. Upon orders, they had blown up the bridge.

When the debris settled, Wierzbowski realized that his patrol had just lost their objective, but he still had no way of informing headquarters. The men agreed with him that there was no point in pulling out of their position. From the sounds that came from the north, they knew a fierce battle continued to rage. Deciding that they still had a job to do at the bridgehead, they preferred to stay and fight.

With a bazooka on his shoulder, accompanied by one of the engineers, Mann crawled forward under covering fire from the remainder of the patrol. About a hundred yards from the defensive position, he located what he thought was an 88-mm-ammunition dump. He fired a bazooka round straight into it.

The ensuing explosion confirmed his suspicions. Hundreds of rounds of exploding shells scattered debris over a wide area. For over an hour Mann and the engineer crawled around in the area of the ammunition dump and sniped at the enemy. They had killed at least six and wounded many more, and were making their way slowly toward one of the 88-mm-gun emplacements when the Germans finally managed to locate them. Rifle and machine-gun fire hailed down on them. Mann was hit twice.

When the firing died, Mann assisted the engineer with the bazooka and they destroyed the 88-mm gun. The enemy renewed its attack as Mann and the engineer raced back to their foxholes. The Germans launched a half-hearted attack. Despite his wounds, Mann picked up his rifle and joined the other defenders in repelling the attack.

A medic finally got to Mann and treated his wounds. The Germans' next concerted attack was successfully beaten back, with high casualties on the enemy side. Their failure seemed to enrage the enemy, and the ring of foxholes in the defensive position came under heavy fire from German artillery, mortars, and machine guns. Several men were wounded. Mann was hit by two more bullets, and the engineer with the bazooka who had accompanied him on the attack was killed.

When the medics finished treating Mann, both his arms were in slings. Wierzbowski ordered him to go back to a safer foxhole, joining the rest of the wounded. Mann requested that he be allowed to stay and demonstrated that he could still use a rifle.

Wierzbowski agreed, though with some reluctance. Even wounded, Mann was one of Wierzbowski's best marksmen.

The medics were now almost out of supplies. Two men, Lieutenant Otto Laier and Staff Sergeant Thomas Betrus, volunteered to get assistance. A few minutes after they left, Betrus came back wounded. He and Laier had been ambushed and Laier had been wounded and taken prisoner.

By mid-afternoon the situation was getting desperate. Wierzbowski considered sending another plea for help. But before he could send out men, two British armored cars appeared on the road on the south side of the canal.

The Germans entrenched around the barracks at the bridge immediately turned their guns on the British vehicles. Pulling behind a building, the armored cars poured a fusillade of accurate fire toward the enemy. Minutes later, the Germans fled to safer positions.

Corporal Daniel Corman left the defensive position and sneaked down to the canal where he located a small boat and rowed across to the south bank. He clambered up to the armored cars and the British gave him most of their medical supplies. Returning to the boat, Corman rowed back across the canal with the much-needed supplies. Shouting across to the commander of the British cars, Wierzbowski requested that the commander get a message to the 101st headquarters concerning the Americans' plight.

The British could not get through. Wierzbowski was on the verge of crossing the river with all his men, but the British advised against it. They could not carry everyone in the two armored cars.

With the armored cars affording some extra fire power, the wounded Mann led a small party around the buildings near the two large gantries and captured a wounded German officer and three German medics. Mann brought them back to the foxholes and ordered the German medics to treat the American wounded, which they did without question.

Shortly afterward, a patrol from E Company managed to get through. The patrol promised to report their situation to battalion headquarters. However, the patrol's message got scrambled. The only information that got to headquarters was that the bridge had been destroyed. Nothing was said about Wierzbowski and his beleaguered men.

As the sun set, the 2nd Platoon of D Company, led by Lieutenant Nicholas Mottla, stumbled into Wierzbowski's position and decided to stay the night. Wierzbowski and Mottla worked out a defensive strategy and Mottla's platoon was sent out to protect one of the original defensive positions.

Reassured that Wierzbowski's group had been relieved, the protecting British armored cars slipped away in the night. The men in Wierzbowski's patrol finally managed to get some sleep. But in the early hours of the morning the Germans launched a massive attack, completely routing Mottla's 2nd Platoon. Mann, considerably weakened from wounds and loss of blood, woke up to see enemy soldiers approaching through the mist.

He yelled a warning. Wierzbowski and Betrus woke up and started hurling grenades. Mann, barely able to fire his rifle, shot four of the enemy who were returning to their defensive position.

The rest of the men, now fully awake, began to repel the enemy. In the fight that ensued, several paratroopers were killed, several more badly wounded. The enemy attack was broken momentarily. But before Wierzbowski could reorganize his position, the Germans came at them again, hurling grenades.

Several grenades that landed in the foxholes were quickly thrown out before they could explode. However, one did explode, and several men were badly injured.

Mann, Lieutenant Wierzbowski, and five other men were in one large foxhole when the Germans started their second rush. A grenade rolled into the bottom of the foxhole. Mann was the only one who saw it. He was leaning against the back of the foxhole, almost too weak to move, when the grenade landed. Yelling a warning, Mann pushed himself off the wall and landed on his back on top of the grenade.

His body took the full force of the explosion. None of the others were injured. Wierzbowski was by his side instantly.

Mann smiled. "My back's gone," he said.

A moment later, he was dead.

Wierzbowski decided that with only three unwounded men left and almost no ammunition, it was futile to struggle on against insurmountable odds. He called a halt to the firing and surrendered to the Germans, who were utterly amazed that such a small group had put up such a fierce fight.

Lieutenant Edward Wierzbowski recommended that Joe Mann be awarded the Medal of Honor. The surviving members of the patrol were in full agreement. Joe Mann, they said, was the bravest soldier they had ever known, and he became the second soldier of the 101st Airborne Division to be awarded the Medal of Honor for his bravery in the face of battle.

6
BATTLEFIELD LOG:
Lima Zulu, Dak Djram Creek, Vietnam, June 1966

Toumorong Mountain is located in Kontum Province on the western edge of the central highlands of Vietnam. On Saturday, June 4, 1966, it became the focal point for "Operation Hawthorne One," a joint U.S. and South Vietnamese Army operation to relieve a small Montagnard outpost. The outpost was manned by a group of local militia known as Trongson, and the entire hamlet held nearly 150 people, the Trongson and their families. Throughout the early part of May, the hamlet had received occasional mortar and sniper fire from the Vietcong, but no serious attempt had been made to overrun the tiny garrison.

However, intelligence information from a "chieu hoi" (a Vietcong deserter, or, to translate literally from the Vietnamese, a "returnee") indicated that the Vietcong intended to take the hamlet in the near future. The jungle area surrounding the mountain was known to be enemy territory. It was subject to frequent bombing by the Air Force in response to calls from the Trongson in the hamlet.

American and Vietnamese commanders in the area

had no intention of allowing the hamlet to be overrun. But at the same time they did not want to establish a Special Forces or Vietnamese Army garrison on the mountain. Meeting in the provincial capital of Kontum, the military commanders decided they would evacuate the hamlet. At the same time, in order not to give the appearance of abandoning the area entirely, they decided to conduct a major sweep to drive out the Vietcong.

The task force assigned to the job was comprised of three Vietnamese battalions, one American battalion, and two American artillery batteries. One Vietnamese Ranger battalion was to sweep toward the foothills of Toumorong from the northwest while two regular Vietnamese Army battalions, accompanied by U.S. Special Forces–trained Civilian Irregular Defense Groups, swept up from the southeast and southwest. The American force, the 2nd Battalion of the 327th Infantry Regiment, 1st Brigade, 101st Airborne, was assigned the task of sweeping the foothills from the north, then proceeding up the mountain to evacuate the hamlet.

The airborne artillery units supporting the operation were the 1st and 2nd Battalions of the 30th Artillery Regiment. The 1st Battalion gun batteries were assigned the task of providing cover for the Vietnamese forces, while Bravo Battery of the 2nd Battalion, under the command of Captain Donald Whalen, was assigned to cover the 1st Battalion from the 327th.

At 0600 hours on June 3, an advance party from the 1st/327th Infantry, under the command of Major David Hackworth, moved by helicopter to their jump-off point, a small clearing to the north of Toumorong called "Landing Zone Jenny." By mid-afternoon the first scout patrols of the advance party had reported that there were no Vietcong in the vicinity of "Jenny." The Artillery commenced an airlift of the remainder of the battalion.

As the sweep operation was not due to begin until the following morning, Hackworth's battalion made camp for the evening in the vicinity of the landing zone. Brigadier General Willard Pearson, Commander of the 1st Brigade, 101st Airborne, decided that the battalion might be somewhat vulnerable near the base of the mountain. Although he knew air support was readily available, he did not want his men to be without artillery covering fire during the night. He ordered that Whalen's gun battery be moved up immediately to provide covering fire.

At 1600 hours, in the main base camp at Dak To, Whalen was informed that his gun battery was to be moved up immediately to the operations area. Whalen ordered the men of his six-gun battery to prepare their newly arrived M-102 105-mm howitzers for rapid deployment to support Hackworth's battalion. Commandeering a Huey gunship, he took off from Dak To and headed for Landing Zone Jenny on a reconnaissance misson.

Whalen intended to set up his guns around the landing zone in order to provide point-blank and close-range fire. Once he saw the location, however, he realized that not only was it somewhat small, it was very wet and muddy. After walking around for a few minutes he decided he could not subject his gunners to the slimy ground conditions.

Whalen ordered the gunship pilot to take off and head toward Dak To. After a few minutes of flying, Whalen located what he considered an ideal gun site close to the Dak Djram Creek. A large, clear area some three and one-half miles to the southwest of Toumorong looked, from the air, almost flat. Whalen ordered the gunship pilot to circle the area for a few moments while he plotted the position of the gun site. He had to be certain that he could adequately cover Hackworth's battalion, both at Landing Zone Jenny throughout the night and during the assault sweep of the mountain during the next few days. Well satisfied that his guns could perform their mission, Whalen ordered the pilot to head back to Dak To.

When the gunship landed at Dak To, Whalen found Captain Ronald Brown, Commander of A Company, 2nd Battalion, 502nd Infantry, waiting at the landing strip. Brown had been hastily ordered to move his 170-man company into whatever location Whalen had chosen and to secure it for the guns. Whalen gave Brown the coordinates of the location, then asked if he and his radio operator could ride with the lead helicopters. Brown was happy to agree. He did not want to end up securing the wrong location, as often happened in the confusing terrain of South Vietnam.

Fifteen Huey "Slick" (UH-1 troop transporters), with Whalen, Brown, and ninety airborne troops on board, lifted off from Dak To, along with an escort of six gunships, and headed toward Whalen's chosen site. In the rush to set up the guns before dark, the landing zone had not been given an official code name. When he was asked for a name, Whalen hastily called it "Landing Zone Lima Zulu."

Arriving over Lima Zulu, the gunships roared in low to check the area. No fire was received. Five Slicks moved in, landing on a narrow trail path alongside the gently sloping site. Airborne troops leaped from the Hueys almost before the landing skids had touched the ground. The soldiers fanned out to form a small defensive perimeter. The remaining helicopters landed in quick succession, disgorged their complements of armed men, then lifted off and headed back to Dak To to collect the remainder of Brown's company.

As the troops fanned out, several men fell into well-concealed pungi-stick pits, favorite traps of the Vietcong. The pits, four or five feet deep, were lined along the bottom with rows of sharpened bamboo sticks tipped with poison. Death was agonizing. Those who survived would suffer severe wounds.

This time, there were no injuries or fatalities. The pits were very old, the pungi sticks rotted through. But the discovery of the pits made the men considerably more cautious. They realized that the enemy had used the area at one time. There was every likelihood of discovering newer, more deadly booby traps.

Once Brown had secured the perimeter of the site, he sent patrols out to scout the surrounding area. One platoon climbed to a small ridge overlooking the site. This platoon would provide covering fire for the helicopters transporting the remainder of his men and Whalen's gun battery.

When further troops arrived, Brown sent another platoon south on a reconnaissance mission toward the position of the Vietnamese battalion and the Special Forces–led defense groups. Brown had received a radio call from one of the Special Forces advisers. He was under attack from a well-concealed 81-mm mortar. The Special Forces soldier was certain that the mortar was located between his own position and Brown's location: he felt that perhaps Brown's men could get to it more quickly. With the Vietnamese group less than half a mile away, Brown decided that he had better silence the enemy mortar, since it could easily be turned against his own gun site.

Listening to Brown's conversations, Whalen saw that

Brown was concerned both for the gun-site security and for the Vietnamese battalion that was under fire. However, Whalen decided it was not really his problem. Brown was accompanied by a forward observer of B Company of the 1st Battalion, 30th Artillery, and it was B Company's responsibility to provide covering fire for the Vietnamese battalion and the Special Forces–led group.

Shortly after the conversation with the Special Forces adviser, the remainder of Brown's company landed. The Slicks were closely followed by four CH-47 Chinooks with the first of Whalen's guns, his command trailer, and his jeep.

Within five minutes, Whalen had one of his six howitzers pointing north toward Hackworth's group and was firing registration rounds under the direction of Hackworth's forward observer on the far side of Toumorong. As the second flight of Chinooks arrived, they were met by light enemy ground fire, but neither Brown nor Whalen could discover where the fire was coming from. Fortunately, no damage was done. The firing ceased once the giant helicopters had unloaded their cargoes.

Whalen intended to set all his guns to cover Hackworth on the other side of Toumorong. But because Brown was concerned about the trouble not half a mile away, on the other side of the hill to the south of their own position, Whalen turned three of the guns around to face the ridge.

During the late evening, Brown's scouting patrols and his outlying perimeter defenders on the ridge came under attack from a large number of enemy soldiers. Fierce fighting took place. Brown was surprised to discover that the enemy soldiers were not just Vietcong.

A large number of regular North Vietnamese Army soldiers were also in the group.

On the far side of the ridge, Vietnamese and Special Forces groups were also under concentrated attack. They were under fire that was much heavier than what Brown's men had been subjected to. The Special Forces adviser informed Brown that he was being attacked by at least a battalion-sized enemy force. It was definitely a regular unit of the North Vietnamese Army.

Whalen and his men listened as their counterparts in B Company, located in the next major valley, fired in support of the embattled troops to the south. They were not called to assist, nor were they called upon to fire toward Toumorong. Hackworth's battalion had made no contact with the enemy.

When morning came, Whalen complied with a request from Brown and the howitzers went into action. Almost forty rounds were unleashed at the ridge where Brown's men had come under attack the night before. The Vietnamese and Special Forces groups maintained that the Vietcong unit that had attacked them had fled toward that ridge. Having fired off his rounds, Whalen turned his guns back toward Toumorong and waited for a fire call from Hackworth.

Hackworth's battalion swept up the mountain without any significant contact with the enemy while Whalen's guns remained silent. On the following day, Monday, June 6, Hackworth evacuated the mountain hamlet and launched a further sweep of the surrounding area. Information from the villagers indicated that a large Vietcong force was somewhere in the area. Hackworth was determined to make contact.

At 1400 hours, forward elements of Hackworth's A Company made contact with a large enemy group at the tiny hamlet of Dak Hanjro on the northwest side of the mountain. Whalen's guns were called into action. As the shells rained down on the hamlet, the remainder of A Company, some distance behind the patrol that had made the first contact, came under heavy fire. Whalen was called upon to split his guns and provide support to both groups.

At the gun battery, Captain Brown, who had now established a good perimeter defense around the guns, was called back to Dak To for some business. He was assured that he would be gone no longer than a day. Brown handed over command of the company to his second-in-command, Lieutenant Karl Beach. After a brief discussion with Whalen, Brown departed.

Whalen received periodic calls for fire support. At 2200 hours he was informed that he would probably not be called again until before dawn the following day. It appeared that the enemy had gone to ground for the night around Hackworth's forces.

At this point Whalen began to wonder what the enemy was doing around Toumorong. He sensed that Vietcong were far more numerous than he had first realized. He was puzzled that the group assaulting Brown's company had not returned.

Brown, Lieutenant Karl Beach, and Whalen had discussed the situation. Whalen knew that the infantry officers were equally puzzled by the brief, ferocious attack that had occurred on their first evening at the gun site. From what Whalen knew of enemy tactics, the enemy should have been back.

Shortly before midnight, Whalen warned his executive officer, Lieutenant Larry Simpson, that the men on duty throughout the night should remain alert, keeping noise and chatter to a minimum. The men were ordered to refrain from using flashlights.

Lieutenant Beach had similar but more positive

thoughts: he was convinced that the enemy would attack the position that night. He had slept throughout the afternoon with the intention of staying awake during the night. Beach organized his company on the extremities of the perimeter and sent his patrols four hundred yards off to the north, west, and south to listen for approaching enemy. The remainder of the company, including a squad of engineers, remained dug in three hundred yards southeast of the battery.

Whalen went to sleep at midnight. His fears were realized two hours later when he was awakened by enemy mortars landing around the gun positions.

Within the span of a few minutes he counted more than twenty rounds exploding inside the security perimeter. Whalen realized that his gun position was being softened up for an infantry attack. By the time he had dressed, the infantry attack had begun.

Gun numbers one, two, four, five, and six formed a rough circle around the number-three gun, which was almost directly in the center. All guns were pointing in a northeasterly direction, toward Toumorong.

Whalen's command post was positioned just south of gun number five. The fire-direction control center was positioned to the east of it, just south of gun number two. Almost due west of the number-five gun was the vehicle park containing five vehicles and guarded by six men under Corporal John Morgan.

As the mortars opened up on the battery, Beach's deployments came under fire. With their attention distracted, a large enemy force slipped through to assault the gun positions.

The main thrust of the enemy attack came from the northwest, directly toward the number-six gun. A secondary attack was directed toward the truck park. Only one platoon was on alert for the night. As the enemy charged, Whalen dashed toward the guns while the remainder of his men staggered from their tents trying to clear the sleep from their numbed minds.

Corporal Morgan and the men at the truck park put up a fierce fight, but they were greatly outnumbered. Morgan shouted to his men to withdraw to the number-five gun position while he remained to cover the retreat. Standing alone, he felled four enemy soldiers who charged straight toward his position.

Out of ammunition, Morgan retreated to the safety of the number-five gun, reloaded his M-16, and started firing at the Vietcong. A savage firefight developed around the number-six gun. The Vietcong charged the gun with a shower of grenades. Sergeant Jerry Carter was killed instantly. Corporal Robert Hemmes was blown backward into a foxhole, landing near Private First Class Larry Cain.

When he saw that Hemmes was badly wounded and that he was alone at the gun pit, Cain slung his M-16 over his shoulder, grabbed Hemmes, and dragged him to the number-three gun, which by now was crowded with defenders.

The North Vietnamese swarmed the number-six gun pit and set up a defensive position. Most of Whalen's men were now in defensive positions around the remaining guns and they were screaming for orders to fire. But Whalen had given strict orders not to fire the howitzers. He knew that almost all of Beach's men were scattered behind the enemy and he had no idea of their exact positions. Repeated attempts to contact Beach by radio had failed. Whalen simply could not take the risk of bringing the deadly howitzers into close-quarter action without a position report from the infantry lieutenant.

The enemy group that had taken the truck park charged the number-five gun pit. They were driven back by a hail of fire. Another mortar barrage started up. This time the 81-mm mortars were accompanied by several 60-mm mortars.

Whalen needed support from headquarters. He raced toward the fire-direction center and was almost there when a 60-mm mortar shell exploded. The fire-direction equipment was wrecked and Whalen was injured in the blast. The fire direction officer, Lieutenant Gerald Forest, and Specialist 5 Mike Walinski, the gunnery "computer," were both wounded.

Whalen ordered Forest and Walinski to remain by the fire-direction center to locate the position of the enemy mortars. He then ordered Specialist 4 Streadback to strap the portable radio to his back and follow him. Whalen raced back to the guns through a hail of enemy fire, with Streadback hard on his heels.

When Streadback raised the artillery operations officer at Dak To, Whalen explained the situation. His men needed support fire, either artillery or air. The operations officer replied that he would attempt to get a Vietnamese artillery unit, located a few miles to the north of their position, to provide fire. He promised he would contact the Air Force for help.

Breaking off with Dak To, Whalen again tried to contact Beach, to no avail. There was heavy firing outside the perimeter and Whalen knew the infantry was under attack. He would have to take a chance and bring his guns into action. He would not inflict any real damage on the enemy, as he would have to shoot high to the west and east, but a bombardment would definitely boost the morale of his own men.

As the howitzers barked in the night, the spirits of the men rose. Whalen allowed them to waste about twenty rounds before calling a halt to the firing. The enemy around number-six gun was preparing to charge Whalen's own position at number three.

A shower of grenades fell around number-three gun as the Vietcong charged. Whalen was hit by a grenade fragment, and the wounded Corporal Hemmes was killed by a bullet. Five other men were wounded in the initial assault, including Whalen's first sergeant, Charles Loveland, and Sergeants Richmond Nail and Malcom Bentz. A fierce, close-combat fight ensued in the darkness. Streadback, the radio operator, operated his M-16 at remarkable speed. He changed magazines so quickly that he was as effective as a machine-gun section.

The enemy pulled back and started to regroup. More North Vietnamese forces joined in the attack on Beach's defensive positions on the perimeter. It became obvious that the enemy was intent on taking the guns before attacking the infantry. In the weird flashing light of gunfire and mortar shell, Whalen could see enemy reinforcements running up to the number-six gun pit.

Just then he heard the drone of an engine. It was Air Force AC-47 "Smokey" gunship, *Puff the Magic Dragon*.

Whalen called for flares and the AC-47 pilot responded immediately. The flares exploded, flooding the gun battery with their eerie light. Whalen saw a horde of enemy advancing. Now, light from the flares gave his men clearly defined targets. Whalen gave the order to fire and emptied his M-16 magazine into three men. The enemy force pulled back, dragging their dead and wounded. Ordering his men to pursue, Whalen raced toward the number-six gun pit. The enemy were routed. The howitzer, now useless, had been hit by at least five hundred bullets and was wrecked beyond repair. But regaining the position fired the gunners with determination.

Enemy bodies were strewn around the gun. As the

last of the North Vietnamese headed for the cover of
nearby brush, the first shells from the Vietnamese
battery to the north ripped through the air.

Whalen could not adjust his guns to hit the enemy
mortars. He contacted the artillery operations officer at
Dak To and asked for the long-range 155-mm guns to
support his position and fire on his command.

Beach's 1st Platoon arrived, sent back by the lieutenant who was concerned about the safety of the guns.
Whalen decided the best position for the platoon was
around the number-five gun facing the truck park. His
judgment was rewarded, as the enemy launched a
ferocious attack straight at number-five gun. Beach's
battle-experienced infantrymen cut the Vietcong to pieces
with well-disciplined fire from M-16s and two M-60
machine guns.

The enemy quickly gave up on number-five gun. A
lull descended. Whalen called for a Med Evac helicopter, which arrived a little before 0400 hours. Eight of
the most severely wounded were loaded into the helicopter, which took off for the hospital at Dak To.
Whalen called for another helicopter but canceled his
call when the enemy launched another massive attack
on the useless number-six gun position.

Sergeant Best and Private First Class Lonnie Bland
fought a rearguard action on the gun, holding their
ground until they had run out of grenades. Almost out
of ammunition, the two men retreated to the number-
three gun. Whalen managed to contact Beach on the
radio and learned where the infantry groups were
positioned.

Around the number-six gun, the enemy had launched
a second assault in greater numbers than before. Whalen
ordered the gunners on number three and number five
to turn their howitzers on the number six position.

They loaded with high explosive shells and awaited his order to fire. The gunners swung their howitzers around and depressed the barrels. Range for number five was fifty yards; range for number three was twenty-five yards: point blank.

Whalen ordered the entire battery to take cover, then roared the fire order for guns three and five. The deadly howitzers recoiled in unison. With the first savage bark of the fusillade, the number-six gun position was almost obliterated. The gunners lifted the barrels slightly. High explosives hurled into the brush behind the remnants of the number-six gun, wiping out enemy troops preparing to launch another attack. Within ten minutes the North Vietnamese had decided they were outmatched. They began their retreat.

Med Evac helicopters arrived to transport the wounded to the hospital in Dak To. The remainder of the men stood by, expecting to receive another attack at first light.

As dawn broke, Whalen saw large numbers of the enemy gathered on two ridges north of his position. As he turned his guns on them, an Air Force AC-47 droned overhead. The pilot informed Whalen he had some twenty thousand rounds of ammunition to spare. He wanted a clear target. Whalen transmitted the enemy position, then watched as the AC-47 unloaded twenty thousand rounds in ninety seconds.

As "Smokey" pulled out of the area, the artillery men at Dak To requested a target. Whalen directed the 155-mm guns along the ridges the gunship had just hosed with 7.62-mm fire. There still appeared to be enemy movement near the top of the ridges. Shortly afterward, a fleet of helicopter gunships arrived. They too were given targets on the hill. They were followed by a formation of Air Force bombers carrying napalm.

Finally, Whalen turned his guns on the ridges and let his gunners fire the last rounds of the battle before Beach's infantry swept the area. Beach's infantry took the ridges without firing a single shot. They discovered the bodies of over two hundred enemy soldiers. The enemy force, well over battalion size, had been wiped out by one battery of airborne gunners-turned-infantrymen and one company of airborne infantry with a handful of airborne combat engineers. Enemy losses outnumbered the 1st Airborne Brigade's by twenty to one. Whalen's guns, "The guns of Lima Zulu," were credited with the victory.

7
Airborne and Aviator Training

Airborne soldiers are no longer simply infantrymen who parachute into battle. They are pilots, air gunners, artillery specialists, missile and weapons systems operators, medical attendants, engineers, and specialists in many other disciplines. Despite the glamour and prestige of the more technically and technologically advanced jobs in a modern army, the job of the front line soldier, the infantryman, is still the most important of all.

If the man on the ground, with a rifle or machine gun in his hand, cannot win and hold territory, there can be no real victory. Despite the never-ending quest for more-advanced weapons and combat equipment, the military brass are well aware of the overriding importance of infantrymen. Consequently, the greater part of the United States Army Airborne is made up of infantry.

Parachuting is almost synonymous with airborne infantry. In the modern Armed Forces a soldier is not considered "Airborne Qualified" until he has completed the Army's course of combat parachute training and has earned his "wings."

Combat parachuting is extremely dangerous. Leaping out of an aircraft traveling at speeds over 120 miles per hour some five hundred feet above the ground—and then relying on a parachute to open correctly—is far from a safe procedure. Nonetheless, military statistics show that parachuting fatalities and serious injuries have been fairly low over the past forty years.

All airborne soldiers are volunteers. For the privilege of volunteering there are rewards and benefits, both personal and material. However, volunteering means taking more risks. And it means giving up the right to say "No sir" a few more times.

The average airborne soldier does not simply leap out of an aircraft. The fact that he is Airborne Qualified mean he has no real choice of when, where, or how he jumps! Loaded with weapons and ammunition, he must also carry a full complement of rations and equipment. Marched into an aircraft and flown to the drop zone, he is ordered to jump out of the aircraft, often into a hail of enemy fire.

His load is supposed to weigh about fifty or sixty pounds, but actual weight is usually closer to one hundred pounds, including utensils, grenades, Claymore Mines, and other explosives. For tactical reasons, combat jumps are usually performed from low altitudes, reducing the time that troops are exposed to adverse winds. From a low altitude, a larger number of troops can be dropped on a specific location in the shortest possible time.

From the airborne soldier's point of view, perhaps the advantage of a low-altitude jump is that it reduces the time he is a defenseless target. To enemy on the ground, a trooper swinging from his parachute risers is an easy shot.

Once out of the aircraft, the airborne soldier must first hope that his parachute will open. It must be fully deployed for a normal descent and landing. As he descends, he must avoid collision with other parachutists. Finally, he must ensure that he lands safely, regardless of the conditions on the landing zone.

Modern parachutes do not usually fail to open. If one does, the soldier can manually deploy the reserve chute strapped just below his chest. However, a normal combat jump is carried out from between five hundred and a thousand feet, and reserve parachutes are not always carried. When they are, considerable speed and skill are required to deploy them quickly enough.

Even if the main parachute deploys normally, gusting winds and a dangerous drop zone threaten the paratroopers. Drop zones may be strewn with rocks, boulders, dense brush, and tree stumps, or fields that are roughly plowed or full of crops such as corn and large cabbage heads, which can cause injuries and even fatalities.

Dangerous drop zones are not the exception. While every attempt is made to select "green fields," or ideal drop zones, battlefield commanders are often forced to accept whatever clear area is available. Airborne soldiers have to take what they are given and make the most of it.

AIRBORNE TRAINING

Every volunteer who is accepted for parachute training travels to Fort Benning, Georgia, to the headquarters of the 4th Airborne Training Battalion for a three-week, basic parachute-training course. Basic parachuting skills are taught to American military personnel and to selected candidates from NATO nations.

Fort Benning has advanced courses for Pathfinders and Jumpmasters, as well as high-altitude-parachuting techniques. The 4th Airborne Training Battalion provides expertise in support of the preparation and review of airborne doctrine for the Army. Members of the battalion make up the Command Exhibition Parachute Team, which demonstrates advanced parachute techniques, tests new parachutes and parachuting equipment, and acts as the commanding general's executive agent for military parachuting.

The basic military parachute course, called "Basic Airborne," is three weeks long. During the first two weeks, each day commences with one hour of physical training for all candidates, male and female, regardless of rank. (Female candidates have some slightly modified physical training exercises, but the time period is the same.) The pace and number of exercises increases throughout the first two weeks, culminating on Friday of the second week with a four-mile run that must be completed in under thirty-five minutes. During the final week, nominal physical training exercises are performed at the start of each day.

The first week of training is called "Ground Week." Most instruction during this week is on an individual basis, ensuring that each student gets the maximum amount of attention. Apart from learning theory, the workings of the parachutes in use today, and how to wear equipment correctly, the following five elements are practiced continuously:

1. Actions of the jumper inside the aircraft.
2. Body control after the jumper leaves the aircraft until opening shock.

3. Control of the parachute during descent.
4. Body control and execution of the parachute landing fall—called the PLF.
5. Parachute control on landing.

Various pieces of equipment are used to teach the five elements mentioned above. The "Mock Door," set at ground level, simulates the interior design of the jump door of an aircraft. Using the Mock Door, paratroopers learn how to don a parachute harness correctly, "shuffle" to the jump door, exit the aircraft in the correct manner, and adopt the proper body position after leaving the aircraft. They also learn to count off the lag time between exit and parachute inflation.

The second apparatus is a thirty-four-foot tower. The exit from this tower, a simulated aircraft door, is thirty-four feet above the ground. Risers from the student's parachute harness are attached to pulleys that simulate the shock of a parachute opening.

During the first week, the student also practices on the "Lateral Drift Apparatus." A wire rope is suspended above the ground with a pulley and handlebar arrangement. One end of the rope is mounted higher than the other. At the high end the student mounts a platform suspended well above the ground. He grabs the handlebars and jumps off. As the pulley runs down the wire, the student approaches the ground just as he would while suspended from a parachute harness under windy conditions. "Lateral" landing techniques, as well as highly dangerous backward landing techniques, can be demonstrated on this apparatus.

A backward landing in combat is to be avoided at all costs, but the technique must be mastered by every student. A lot of training time is spent on the "Lateral Drift Apparatus" in order to reduce the injury rate sustained on landings.

The second week of the Basic Airborne Course is called "Tower Week." "Mass Exit" techniques are taught, and trainees practice further on the "Swing Training Ladder," the "Suspended Harness," the "Wind Machine" and the "250-Foot Free Tower."

On the "Swing Training Ladder" the student is suspended from a harness that is swung back and forth before being released. Upon release, the student must use correct landing technique. As proficiency is developed, the harness is raised. Drop heights become greater as the student progresses.

In the "Suspended Harness," the student learns how to make a safe exit from his harness if he lands in tall trees, among high-tension wires, or in deep water.

The "Wind Machine" is a device that creates high winds, teaching the student how to control his billowing parachute on the ground. He also learns how to free himself from the chute when landing in windy conditions.

The "250-Foot Free Tower" is the final test. The student dons a deployed parachute, with the top of the parachute attached to a line suspended from one of the four booms. The line is hauled in. The parachute, with the student hanging in the harness, is pulled up to the top of the tower, then released. This is effectively the student's first parachute drop.

As the chute speeds toward the ground, the parachutist must control the descent, then demonstrate proper landing technique, parachute release, and recovery upon reaching the ground. Each student is dropped twice from the tower before the end of the second week of training. During each drop, he must satisfy his instructors that he is sufficiently prepared to progress to an aircraft jump.

The third week of the course is called "Jump Week." It starts with a review of parachute malfunctions and familiarization with the type of aircraft that will be used to make the first jump. After students make their first jump, they are awarded their "wings." But the course is not over. To finish, they must make another four jumps, one of which must be completed at night. After that, they are considered "Airborne Qualified."

ARMY AVIATORS

Warrant officers and officer candidates who wish to be pilots must meet the academic and military standards stated in Army Regulations before they are accepted for pilot training. Candidates are sent to Fort Rucker, Alabama, to the Army Aviation Training Brigade, where they commence the "Initial Entry Rotary Wing Aviator Course," lasting approximately nine months.

The majority of the course is some sixteen weeks long. Students spend a considerable amount of time in classrooms, or "ground school," as it is sometimes called, learning subjects such as the theory and principles of flight and navigation, as well as details about helicopter engines and airframes, aircraft weight and balance, and meteorology.

After an initial period of classroom work, flight training commences. Training is conducted in the Hughes TH-55A Osage helicopter. By the end of the first sixteen weeks, all successful candidates will be proficient in flying this machine and will progress to the "advanced" portion of their training. Advanced training begins with a transition from the TH-55A to the UH-1 Iroquois, more commonly called the "Huey." Along with advanced flight training there is further classroom work and written exams.

At the end of the nine-month course, candidates take

a series of written and practical tests. If the required minimum standards are achieved, candidates will graduate as "Rated Army Aviators" who are assigned to operational units. They remain at Fort Rucker to undergo transitional training, learning to operate a specific type of helicopter. (At this point some pilots will begin transition training from rotary wing to fixed wing; most of this training also takes place at Fort Rucker.)

Time spent on transition training varies with the type of helicopter or fixed-wing aircraft. When the course is completed, the pilot will finally join his unit, where he starts training again, learning the specific mission role of the unit.

Training never really ends. New tactics, updated equipment, and changing operations requirements will require the aviator to take refresher courses throughout his career in the Army.

8
BATTLEFIELD LOG:
Corregidor Island, February 16, 1945

The 101st and 82nd Airborne Divisions are perhaps the most famous of all American airborne fighting units. Having earned their battle honors in Europe and North Africa, these divisions have been justifiably praised for their gallantry and heroism during World War II.

Equally gallant were the actions of the 11th Airborne Division in the Pacific Theater. Although the 11th Airborne deserves as much public acclaim as the 101st and 82nd, the men of the 11th are often neglected in the history books simply because they were operating in the Pacific Theater. To most people, the war in the Pacific is associated with the Marines and the Navy.

Generally, war correspondents gave little attention to Army actions during the "island seizing" campaign in the Pacific. Most of the war correspondents of the day wanted to be with the Marines, who spearheaded the Pacific campaign.

On several occasions, islands were recaptured without the use of the Marines: the spearhead troops were airborne soldiers and Army infantry. One such island was Corregidor, at the entrance to Manila Bay on the main Philippine island of Luzon. This was the Island where General Douglas MacArthur made his last stand against the invading Japanese in 1942.

Corregidor was a fortress island that had been surrendered to Commodore George Dewey by the Spanish after he destroyed their fleet in Manila Bay on April 1, 1898. Island defenses were so formidable that Dewey was forced to sneak the American fleet past Corregidor in the dead of night. The commander of the island garrison saw his nation's great fleet destroyed by Dewey, without the loss of one American vessel. He immediately surrendered.

Forty-four years later, in May 1942, Lieutenant General Jonathan Wainwright surrendered Corregidor to the Japanese. But it was not given up easily. After a bloody attempt to hold the tiny island, Wainwright, who had been left in command when MacArthur was ordered to leave by President Roosevelt, conceded defeat. It had become obvious that his mixed group of defenders—some four thousand sailors, soldiers, marines, airmen, and civilians—were hopelessly outnumbered and could not be reinforced.

The island is shaped like a tadpole, with its "head" pointing to the west and its "tail" curving back to the southeast. From head to tail it is three and one-half miles long. The "head" or main part is roughly one and one-half miles in diameter. The "tail" is about two miles long and no more than one thousand yards wide, tapering down to a point at its southeast extremity.

At the head is a tabletop mountain with almost sheer sides that rise some five hundred fifty feet from the sea. This area was named "Topside" by the Americans shortly after they acquired it from the Spanish. Sloping down toward the tail is an area about one hundred feet below Topside named "Middleside." Just below it, where the tail joins the body of the island, the remaining part of the island is called "Bottomside." About one thousand yards east of Middleside, Bottomside rises to four hundred feet in a humplike hill. This hump is called Malinta Hill. From here, the high ground slopes down to the relatively flat and sandy tip of the island.

A large barracks complex was constructed in the center of Topside. Just south of it was a rectangular parade ground measuring 250 by 300 yards. Southeast of the parade ground was a nine-hole golf course 350 yards long by 180 yards wide.

A road tunnel through Malinta Hill allowed access from Topside to a tiny airstrip, Kindley Field, on the east end of the island. Inside Malinta Hill were underground storage facilities and living quarters as well as a small hospital. In this underground complex MacArthur had established his headquarters before being ordered to leave by Roosevelt.

Another underground complex, carved out in Bottomside, was named "Radio Intercept Tunnel." Built in 1939, it was used to house special radio equipment. A team of operators, whose sole function was to intercept and decode Japanese radio messages, was posted in this base. Intercepted enemy messages provided U.S. Naval Commanders with vital information and contributed significantly to the defeat of the Imperial Japanese Navy at the Battle of Midway.

By February 3, 1945, the Japanese on the main island of Luzon were almost beaten. General MacArthur directed that an assault be launched on Corregidor Island. Enemy defenders were making a nuisance of themselves, bombarding supply ships heading into the bay for the capital, Manila. The enemy had inflicted casualties on the ships, despite continual shelling of the fortress by the Air Force and the Navy. The bombardment had gone on for almost two months.

MacArthur ordered Sixth Army Headquarters to plan a combined amphibious-parachute assault on the island. The task of leading the assault was assigned to thirty-three-year-old Colonel George Jones, Commander of the 503rd Airborne Regiment Combat Team (sometimes referred to as the 503rd Parachute Regimental Combat Team).

The three battalions of the 503rd were a battle-seasoned force that had seen action in New Guinea and Noemfoor Island. They had been part of the assault force that landed on Mindoro Island, to the south of Luzon, but had encountered no enemy resistance on landing. Assigned to defend the airstrip on Mindoro while other units were sent inland to the north of the island, they were getting restless. Then the call came for them to take Corregidor.

Jones was given a battle-experienced infantry battalion, the 3rd Battalion of the 34th Infantry Regiment, under the command of Lieutenant Colonel Edward Postlethwaite, to carry out the amphibious portion of the operation. On the airborne side he was assigned Company C of the 161st Airborne Engineer Battalion, and Batteries A, B, and C of the 462nd Parachute Field Artillery. The assault force, named the "Rock Force," was only a four-battalion unit. Sixth Army Intelligence had determined that there were between 250 and 700 enemy on the island: four fighting battalions were considered sufficient "overkill" to wipe them out.

Unfortunately, as Jones would find out, the intelligence estimates were wrong. There were 5,100 enemy soldiers then on Corregidor under the command of Captain Ijn Itagaki. These included a mix of Army, Navy, and civilian personnel. But the majority of the defenders were fierce Imperial Japanese Marines who had received orders from Tokyo to defend the island to the last man.

Although they erred in their estimate of enemy strength on the island, the intelligence men provided excellent topographical information to Jones. From thousands of photographs and maps of the island, they constructed a large, highly detailed model using papier-mâché, sand, chicken wire, wood, cardboard, stones, and soil. This model they presented to Jones. It was an impressive mock-up that proved to be an incredible asset in the planning of the operation.

"D" Day was set for February 16. On February 6, Jones went aloft in a reconnaissance bomber of the Fifth Army Air Force to have a look at the island. Reconnaissance aircraft joined a formation of bombers on their daily bombing run, and Jones had a good look at the island from the air.

After several passes, Jones realized the risk involved. Despite the light estimate of enemy defenders, a parachute assault on Corregidor appeared to be an ambitious and dangerous undertaking.

After the reconnaissance flight Jones returned to the model for a second look. It was obvious that the best place for a parachute drop was the flat, sandy area of Bottomside around Kindley Field. But Bottomside was too far away from the Japanese main defensive positions.

The other obvious place was Topside. But only two areas could be used as drop zones, the parade ground or the golf course. The area around both of these potential drop zones was a mass of splintered trees and jagged concrete structures left behind after heavy bombing by the Fifth and Thirteenth Army Air Forces and shelling by Navy battleships. Both zones were close to the five-hundred-foot-high cliffs. If the wind dragged a parachutist over the edge, he would either die on the rocks below or drown in the waters at the mouth of Manila Bay.

Jones estimated that casualties would exceed fifty percent in what would later be called the "worst drop zones in World War II."

The 317th Troop Carrier Group, under the command of Colonel John Lackey, was assigned the difficult task of getting the 503rd onto Corregidor. Lackey informed Jones that he had only fifty-one C-47 aircraft available. Each would carry one battalion. There would be a six-second "window" over each of the tiny drop zones.

The wind on Topside held steady at around 25 miles per hour. If the aircraft flew over the island, five hundred feet above the ground, at a speed of about 125 miles per hour, between six and eight men could jump from each aircraft with some chance of survival.

Jones decided he would drop two of his battalions with supporting units of the Engineers and Airborne Artillery on "D" Day and hold the remaining battalion in reserve for "D" Day plus one. He and Lackey formulated a plan: the aircraft would fly a northeasterly course over the island in two parallel columns about one thousand feet apart. Each aircraft would drop six men, then swing around and join the tail of the column to make second, third, and fourth passes. After all the men had jumped, the planes would return to Mindoro to pick up the next battalion.

Jones chose his 3rd Battalion, under the command of Lieutenant Colonel John Erickson, to make the initial drop. The 3rd was reinforced with the company from the 161st Engineer Battalion, Battery D of the 462nd Airborne Artillery (more commonly called the Parachute Field Artillery). Also included in the first drop was Jones with several members of his headquarters staff as well as the headquarter's radio operators and their equipment.

Once on the ground, Jones knew, Erickson's battalion would have to hold on to the drop zones for five hours before Lackey's C-47 transporters could bring in the next battalion, the 2nd Battalion of the 503rd, under the command of Major Lawson Caskey. Caskey's battalion would be accompanied by the remainder of the 503rd's headquarter's staff and Battery B of the 462nd Airborne Artillery. The 2nd Battalion would then assist Erickson's 3rd as they cleared out of the drop zones and gained more ground.

The third and final drop on Topside, to be made on "D" Day plus one, would be handled by the 1st Battalion under the command of Major Roberts "Pug" Woods, accompanied by Battery A of the 462nd Airborne Artillery.

For the amphibious part of the operation Jones planned to land Postlethwaite's infantry on Blacks Beach on the south shore of Bottomside. Postlethwaite's battalion would begin their amphibious assault after the paratroopers dropped. Jones hoped Postlethwaite could provide covering fire to assist the infantry during its landing operation.

At dawn on February 16, eight cruisers and fourteen destroyers launched a savage bombardment. Shortly afterward, two dozen B-24 Liberators bombed Topside. They were joined by eleven B-25 Mitchell bombers concentrating on the south side of Topside. Navy shelling ceased one minute before Lackey's transporters reached the island: during that minute, twenty-five A-20 Havoc attack bombers made low-level bombing and strafing runs over the drop zones and the rest of the island.

When the leading C-47 flew over the drop zone, Erickson led an eight-man "stick" out the door at a fast pace. Instantly he realized the wind was stronger than expected. He and his men would land some two hundred yards south of their target. Jones, watching the operation from a circling C-47 piloted by Lackey, called to the Jumpmasters in the other aircraft to delay their jumps for a few seconds. Lackey's pilots were told to descend another hundred feet to give the parachutists a better chance at the clear drop zones. This accomplished, Lackey swung his aircraft into the line for a pass over the drop zone. Jones watched as the first "stick" floated down. Again he called for the Jumpmasters of the following aircraft to delay their drops. By the time Lackey brought the C-47 around for a second pass, Jones was satisfied that the timing was as close as possible. He instructed Lackey to make another pass. Jones said he would jump with the remaining five men in the aircraft, as he felt that he had accomplished everything possible from the air.

As his parachute blossomed, Jones saw he was drifting badly to the south. He pulled hard on his parachute risers to spill air and offset the drift. Nearing the ground, he spotted a small, clear space between a mass of tangled concrete and a splintered tree. Aiming for the space, Jones missed the concrete tangle but hit the splintered tree. A large sliver penetrated deep into his right thigh. Releasing his parachute, he gritted his teeth and yanked the splinter from his leg. Then he went to the assistance of his orderly, who had broken his ankle when he landed.

The Japanese defenders were completely surprised by the airborne assault. Moments after the first landing, the island commander, Captain Itagaki, and his entire comand-post staff were wiped out by a hand grenade tossed by one of the paratroopers.

In just over an hour, the battalion was on the ground. But before the last man landed, Erickson gathered his men together to seize the old Topside barracks. There was a short skirmish with the enemy. Two enterprising paratroopers, Sergeant Frank Arrigo and Private First Class Clyde Bates, found the only telegraph pole on Topside that had not been destroyed. Amid a hail of sniper fire, they climbed the tower and unfurled "Old Glory."

By 10:00 A.M. the 3rd Battalion held firm control over the area around the barracks. Amid constant sniper fire, patrols were sent out to assess the enemy positions. They encountered heavy resistance from well-entrenched enemy soldiers.

Jones moved his .50-caliber machine guns into position as Postlethwaite's amphibious force hit the beach. At 10:30, behind a barrage of Navy rocket fire, Postlethwaite came ashore. Hidden Japanese machine guns opened up on the landing infantry. When Jones opened fire above and behind them, the Japanese were silenced. Postlethwaite's battalion came ashore with minimum casualties, only two dead and six wounded.

Postlethwaite led his men to the top of Malinta Hill and positioned a few tanks and howitzers near the beachhead. His men encountered very little resistance.

By noon, Jones was satisfied with the progress of the assault. Postlethwaite's battalion was digging in on top of Malinta Hill and Erickson's battalion was quite established around the shelled-out Topside barracks. Because of the light resistance, Jones considered cancelling the drop of the 2nd Battalion. He was certain the 2nd would suffer casualties in the treacherous drop zones, and he wanted to hold the battalion in reserve if possible. However, Jones still didn't know the enemy on Topside. He decided to proceed with the drop as scheduled.

Shortly before 1300 hours, Lackey's transporters appeared over the island to drop Caskey's 2nd Battalion. By 1345 hours the entire battalion and its supporting artillery was on the ground. Like Erickson's 3rd Battalion, it had suffered about sixteen percent casualties.

Organizing his men, Caskey took over the drop zones and began clearing areas to the south. Erickson's battalion moved out to secure the remainder of Topside. They met with only isolated pockets of resistance. Not expecting a parachute assault on the island, the Japanese had established their heaviest defenses along the approaches from Middleside to Topside and on the eastern end of Malinta Hill.

By nightfall Jones was confident that Topside was secure. He radioed Sixth Army Headquarters, canceled the air drop of Major Woods's 1st Battalion, and instructed the battalion to fly from Mindoro to the Subic Bay Airstrip. There they were to board the landing craft that would bring them to the island the following afternoon.

Shortly after dark, bands of Japanese soldiers crawled out of their caves on Topside and Malinta Hill to attack the dug-in paratroopers and infantry. Several bloody encounters took place. The enemy soldiers would accept no quarter. The fighting stopped just before dawn, and as first light appeared the paratroopers peered out of their foxholes around Topside to see the area littered with scores of dead.

Twenty-one-year-old Private Lloyd McCarter, who had given up his rank of sergeant to join the paratroopers in August 1942, had dug a secure foxhole slightly to the west of Topside barracks, close to some half-ruined administration buildings. He counted eleven bodies, nine of which had fallen before his own gun. Clambering out of the foxhole, he started to clear away the bodies when a sniper opened fire. He raced in the direction of the sniper's position and took cover behind a large rock.

He waited for a few moments, then casually stood up. McCarter dived flat as the sniper fired again. Now McCarter had pinpointed his attacker. He crawled to within a few feet of the concealed enemy and calmly shot him through the head.

Minutes after McCarter returned to his foxhole, another sniper opened fire. McCarter again stood up in full view to locate where the enemy was concealed. When the sniper fired, McCarter took cover, then set off at a fast crawl toward the sniper's position.

Moments later, McCarter's colleagues heard a burst from his machine gun followed by a loud scream from the sniper. McCarter waited a few moments, crawled to the sniper's position to confirm the kill, then returned to his own foxhole. To the amazement of his fellow soldiers, McCarter repeated the performance four more times during the morning, each time exposing himself to draw sniper fire. He was finally ordered to stop by his platoon leader, who was worried that he would lose his best soldier in the deadly game.

The 1st Battalion was ordered to make a beach landing at Subic Bay. As they approached Blacks Beach, the landing craft were greeted by a hail of heavy-caliber enemy fire pouring down from concealed positions in caves on the slopes of Topside. The barrage lasted only a few minutes, but before the firing ceased, six men had been killed. The landing craft were riddled with holes.

Caskey led his men through steep ravines to Middleside, then up Topside to join the rest of the 503rd. Jones ordered Caskey to have his men dig in and act as a reserve unit for the 2nd and 3rd Battalions.

Throughout the day there had been occasional sniper fire and infrequent contact with small groups of enemy. As darkness descended, the firing ceased. At midnight fifty enemy soldiers emerged from their caves to mount a suicidal "Banzai" charge against Postlethwaite's infantry on Malinta Hill. Fifteen minutes after the attack began, thirty-six Japanese Marines were dead. The remainder sought shelter in their caves.

At 0300 hours another "Banzai" attack was launched against the infantry by a force of three hundred Japanese. Fighting continued until late afternoon. From their positions on Topside the paratroopers dealt with the small number of enemy who charged at their positions.

All was quiet on the night of February 18. At 0600 hours, the morning of February 19, paratroopers on Topside heard a low chanting coming from behind the old administration buildings west of the barracks. The chanting accelerated quickly into frantic cries of "Banzai!" Almost six hundred Imperial Japanese Marines suddenly appeared from the buildings and tangled shrub growth. Paratroopers who were just waking up or going about their daily ablutions were taken completely by surprise.

McCarter was one of the few paratroopers who was prepared. The spearhead of the Japanese attack was aimed almost directly at his foxhole. He stood up and opened fire with his machine gun. Enemy soldiers fell like pins under a bowling ball. McCarter changed magazines with lightning speed. Halfway through the sixth magazine, the gun overheated and jammed.

A Japanese soldier bayonet-charged. McCarter sidestepped, parried the thrust, and clubbed the crazed soldier. As a second Japanese advanced, McCarter hurled his red-hot weapon, catching the soldier full in the face. The enemy fell to his knees. McCarter dived into the foxhole and yanked a Browning automatic from the grasp of a dead paratrooper. Turning on the Japanese, he finished the soldier with a short burst of fire.

More of the enemy were surging forward. Bullets whined around McCarter as he opened fire. He stood his ground, pouring round after round into the Imperial Forces. Some enemy fell not three feet from the barrel of the machine gun. McCarter was soon surrounded by a stack of bodies.

When the Browning overheated, he hurled it at the advancing enemy and scrambled toward another foxhole.

The foxhole was occupied by a dead soldier. McCarter seized the man's M-1 and leaped up to meet the next wave of the assault. Eighteen enemy soldiers fell before the blazing M-1, most within a few feet of the foxhole. McCarter climbed over the bodies to seek out further targets. Four more soldiers fell beneath his deadly fire before a sniper's bullet caught him in the middle of the chest, slamming him to the ground.

A medic saw him fall. McCarter struggled to his feet, and the medic tried to pull him to safety. But McCarter persuaded the medic to leave him where he was. Propping himself up on a pile of the dead, he continued the fight, at the same time shouting warnings to his colleagues.

Fierce hand-to-hand fighting occurred all around him and in nearby foxholes. Lying on top of the enemy bodies, McCarter killed another fifteen men before he finally lost consciousness and crumpled up in a pool of his own blood. The medic saw him slump over and crawled toward him. McCarter was still alive. The medic dragged him to the safety of another foxhole and started to work on his wound.

When the firing finally stopped, the area around the paratroopers' foxholes presented a gruesome sight. Five hundred Japanese Marines were sprawled to the west of the 503rd's defensive position. Nearly a hundred lay in front of the foxholes that McCarter had occupied.

Thirty-three paratroopers were killed during the suicidal attack and seventy-five wounded. McCarter's colleagues and the company commander, who had witnessed
his incredible actions, insisted that he be taken down to
the beach immediately and transported to one of the
hospital ships for surgery. McCarter was returned to
the United States, to Letterman Army Hospital in San
Francisco, where he received a personal letter from
President Truman inviting him to visit the White House.
After several months of recuperating, McCarter was
pronounced fit to travel. At the White House, President Truman presented him with the Medal of Honor.

Colonel Jones, his paratroopers, and the infantry
spent the next eight days clearing out the remaining
Japanese on the island. Four thousand dead were counted.
Only twenty prisoners were taken. American casualties
numbered four hundred fifty, and one thousand were
wounded. Although there had been numerous acts of
gallantry and valor, only one Medal of Honor was
awarded to the "Rock Force." All who witnessed
McCarter's actions were of one opinion—if he had not
put up such a tremendous fight, many more Americans
would have lost their lives on Corregidor.

General MacArthur arrived on Corregidor on March
2, 1945, landing in a Navy PT boat, the same way he
had left almost three years earlier. Before MacArthur's
arrival, the flag that Sergeant Arrigo and Private Bates
had risked their lives to hoist up the telegraph pole was
quickly lowered. It was well known that MacArthur did
not like unofficial flag-raising ceremonies. When he had
spoken to the troops, MacArthur ordered a flag to be
hoisted on the old flagpole by the parade ground.
Although somewhat bent and splintered, that flagpole
was still standing.

Prior to the battle on Corregidor, the 503rd's regimental patch was a snarling wildcat suspended from an open parachute. A few weeks after leaving the island, one of the paratroopers designed a new patch. It shows the island of Corregidor outlined in red with a large white eagle about to attack.

That patch remains the official insignia of the 503rd to the present day.

9
BATTLEFIELD LOG:
Los Banos Prison Camp,
February 23, 1945

On January 31, 1945, the commander of the 11th Airborne Division, Major General Joseph Swing, sent his troops into battle on the island of Luzon. Swing had three regiments at his disposal—the 187th and 188th Glider Infantry Regiments and the 511th Parachute Infantry Regiment—a total of eight thousand men. Swing's division was ordered to land at Nasugbu, south of Manila Bay. At the same time, the 1st Cavalry and 38th Infantry Divisions were to land north of Manila Bay. Once ashore, the cavalry and the infantry would turn south and fight their way to the capital city, Manila. The 11th Airborne Division would turn north to attack the city from the south flank. This pincerlike movement was planned to cause confusion among the Japanese defenders. If they held back their reserves until they learned where the American assault was coming from, attacking forces would have the upper hand. Lieutenant General Robert Eichelberger, Eighth Army Commander, hoped to accomplish two things with this plan. First, he wanted the infantry and the airborne to gain a firm foothold on land before the Japanese threw all their might against them. Second, he hoped the Japanese would split up their reserves.

General Swing divided his three regiments into two groups for the initial assault. Sending the 187th and 188th Glider Infantry Regiments to land on the beaches south of Nasugbu, he ordered the 511th to make a parachute drop a short distance inland on Tagaytay Ridge. Route 17 ran east from Nasugbu around Tagaytay Ridge and then north to Manila. Swing knew that the Japanese were dug in on the ridge and that they could control the road and slow up the advance of his forces. By dropping the 511th on top of the ridge, he hoped the Japanese would be taken by surprise. The 511th could knock out their gun positions before the advancing glider infantry approached.

The plan worked well. The 11th moved rapidly toward Manila. By February 4 they were just south of the city, where they encountered the Japanese defensive line of pill boxes and dugouts, the "Genko Line" (named after the Japanese commander who conceived the idea).

Swing's forces launched their assault on the line in an attempt to take Nichols Field, the airfield just south of the capital, and the old garrison of Fort McKinley, which was heavily defended by the Japanese. Responding to a top-secret signal from General MacArthur's headquarters, Swing detached some of his troops from the fighting and prepared them for an airborne assault on a prison camp at Los Banos. His orders called for the rescue of over two thousand American military families from the camp. But when he discovered that the camp was almost fifty miles behind the enemy lines, Swing objected strongly.

Calling in to headquarters, Swing pointed out that he had barely enough men to smash through the defenses

on the Genko Line. He might take the airfield and Fort
McKinley, but he did not think that he could mount a
rescue mission with a mere handful of troops. For that
he would need at least two battalions. Swing requested
that he be allowed to take both Nichols Field and Fort
McKinley before considering a rescue mission.

Eighth Army Headquarters granted his request, but
advised him to make plans for the rescue mission as
soon as the airfield was taken. General Swing then
ordered his intelligence officer, Lieutenant Colonel Henry Muller, to start gathering information on the Los
Banos prison camp. Los Banos (meaning "the baths") is
a small town on the southwestern shore of Laguna de
Bay, the largest freshwater lake on Luzon. The lake is
southeast of Manila, in an area that was firmly in
Japanese hands. Muller discovered that the prison camp—
an agricultural college before the Japanese occupation—
was only a short distance inland from the town. It held
some 2,147 prisoners—men, women, and children—and
a considerable number of missionaries, nuns, clergy-
men, and priests.

Filipino guerrillas provided Muller with information
on the town of Los Banos and the surrounding area. To
his dismay, Muller learned that there were between
nine thousand and fifteen thousand Japanese troops
north of the camp. They were within four hours' travel
of Los Banos.

One piece of information particularly excited Muller.
An American engineer, Peter Miles, had recently es-
caped from the camp and the guerrillas knew where he
was located. Miles was contacted and brought to Swing's
headquarters. Miles proved invaluable, as he had an
almost photographic memory. Drawing a detailed map
of the prison camp, he gave the location of all the

Japanese guard posts, administration buildings, supply stores, living quarters, and recreational areas.

Reconnaissance photographs confirmed everything on Miles's drawing. But perhaps the most important information he provided was the exact number of enemy guards at the camp as well as the number of prisoners, their states of health, and their locations within the camp compound. Miles knew by heart the ritualistic daily routine that the Japanese enforced. By February 15, Muller had gathered enough information to enable General Swing to set his operations officer to work formulating a plan of attack.

By then, Swing's forces had overrun Nichols Field and were battling with stubborn enemy groups still trying to hold the area. Fort McKinley, under attack from two divisional regiments, proved to be a difficult target. It was extremely well defended. Other units of the 11th were in the outskirts of Manila, engaged in vicious street fighting with the enemy. The Japanese, as usual, would give no ground. Their defensive positions could be taken by the 11th Airborne only after savage fighting. There was no surrender, only death at the hands of the enemy, or suicide, and the men of the 11th knew it was pointless trying to be merciful. For each man it was kill or be killed.

By February 17, Eighth Army Headquarters again put pressure on Swing for the prison-camp rescue. HQ was concerned that the Japanese might murder the prisoners en masse since their battle to hold the island was going badly. Swing reluctantly agreed with his superiors. He ordered his operations officer to prepare a plan of attack.

From the beginning the planners realized that the rescue operation would be dangerous and difficult. The best plan would require flawless timing, astute leadership, and considerable secrecy—otherwise, the entire operation would turn into a disaster.

When the final draft was placed in front of General Swing, the operations officers added a note that the leaders would have to be carefully chosen. Studying the plan, Swing realized why. It called for a simultaneous three-pronged assault, one by air, one by land, and one by water. The four major fighting elements included a reconnaissance/guerrilla unit, an amphibious assault unit, a parachute assault unit, and an infantry assault unit.

The plan called for the 11th Airborne Division's reconnaissance unit of thirty men—and a small group of Filipino guerrillas, under the command of a brilliant reconnaissance officer, Lieutenant George Skau—to sail down the lake in ten native canoes two nights prior to D Day. Skau would land the canoes to the east of Los Banos and hide his reconnaissance unit in the jungle until the following night. On the morning of February 23, he would leave a handful of his men near the beaches by Los Banos, moving the remainder into position around the prison camp. His mission was to silently kill any enemy in posts in the surrounding area.

In the meantime, one company of the 511th would fly down from Nichols Field and parachute in to join up with Skau and a battalion-sized force from the 511th. Supporting airborne artillery would travel down the lake in amphibious tractors (amphtracs) to land on the beaches by Los Banos. Part of the battalion would stay on the beaches with the artillery; the remainder would drive the amphtracs up the road to camp. Loaded on the amphtracs, the prisoners would return across the lake to safety. The amphtracs would then collect the reconnaissance patrol, the parachute company, the remainder of the 511th, and the supporting artillery.

In order to confuse the enemy, one battalion of the

188th Glider Infantry would start south from Manila along Route 1, which ran along the shores of the lake to Los Banos, on the night of February 22. This battalion would race to the town of Mamatid near the shores of the lake. Early on the morning of D Day, it would battle its way toward Los Banos, ten miles farther south. The 188th's part of the operation was diversionary. It would withdraw to Manila as soon as the prisoners and rescue forces had retreated from Los Banos. However, in the event that the amphtracs were unable to return to Los Banos to collect the 511th and the reconnaissance unit, the 188th would attempt to hold their ground until the rescue team fought their way overland to link up with them.

Although the plan required perfect coordination and timing, it was brilliant. The concept was accepted by General Swing, who passed it along to Corps headquarters for approval. Lieutenant General Oscar Griswold, commander of XIV Corps of the Eighth Army and Swing's immediate superior, readily approved the plan. From MacArthur's headquarters Swing received his authority to proceed with the plan. Within twenty-four hours after submitting the plan to Griswold, Swing called in his selected leaders.

On the afternoon of February 20, Lieutenant John Ringler, a young company commander of the 1st Battalion of the 511th, was ordered to leave his unit and return to the division command post at Paranaque. Ringler's unit was engaged in heavy fighting against well-entrenched Japanese units. He informed the messenger that headquarters would simply have to wait: he had no intention of leaving his unit at that particular moment.

The messenger departed. Shortly afterward, a senior officer arrived in a jeep with a military police escort.

He informed Ringler that General Swing wanted to see him immediately.

Without protest, Ringler climbed into the jeep. He was unshaven, covered in sweat, dirt, dust- and blood-smeared, after almost two weeks of continuous hard fighting. When he arrived at the command post, he was informed of his part in the rescue attempt. After the operation had been fully explained to him, he was ordered to return to the front line. His company would withdraw immediately to Nichols Field to prepare for a parachute drop on Los Banos on the morning of February 23.

Ringler ordered his men to withdraw. His battalion commander, Lieutenant Colonel Henry Burgess, was ordered to pull back the remainder of his tired and battered battalion and report to headquarters. Burgess relocated his men at a campsite near Paranaque, then reported to the command post. He was informed that Ringler's company would make a parachute drop on Los Banos. The remainder of the battalion would be taken on board amphtracs and transported by road to the town of Mamatid. The amphtracs would enter the water in the early hours of the morning of February 23. Battery D of the 457th Parachute Field Artillery would be assigned to Burgess, who would land on the beaches to provide supporting fire.

As Burgess was being briefed, Colonel Joseph Gibbs, commander of the 672nd Amphibious Tractor Battalion, moved his entire battalion from the northern side of Manila down to Paranaque. Gibbs led his unit on a wild ride through the streets of the ravaged city, fighting most of the way. Arriving in the command-post area early on the morning of February 22 with fifty-nine serviceable amphtracs, he prepared his vehicles for the amphibious side of the operation.

While the amphtracs were battling their way down to Paranaque, Colonel John Lackey, commander of the 317th Troop Carrier Group, provided aircraft from one of his best squadrons to perform the air drop. Lackey allocated the task to the 65th Troop Carrier Squadron. He volunteered to lead the squadron, but he pointed out that his aircraft could not possibly land at Nichols Field. The runways were full of bomb craters. Engineers told him that it would be some time before the airstrip was operational. Swing assured Lackey that within twenty-four hours a runway would be available at Nichols Field. He contacted the engineers and ordered them to prepare a landing strip.

Colonel "Shorty" Soule, commander of the 188th Glider Infantry Regiment, was the last unit commander to be contacted. He sent his 1st Battalion, under the command of the brilliant Lieutenant Colonel Ernest La Flamme, for the diversionary attack down Route 1. La Flamme pulled his fighting gliderman back from the streets of Manila on the night of February 20 to give them a rest period. His company commanders wanted a reason for the withdrawal, but La Flamme could not tell them; only he and one of his senior officers were permitted to know the exact details of the operation.

When darkness fell, on February 21, Lieutenant Skau led his reconnaissance patrol and a handful of guerrillas to the shores of Laguna de Bay. At 1900 hours they boarded ten native canoes and set out south toward Los Banos. It took Skau some considerable time to coordinate the paddlers so that the splashing noise of paddles was kept to a minimum. In near silence, the long canoes glided down the lake.

It was a moonless night. In the darkness, the flat shoreline was invisible. With nothing more than a compass, a watch, and a primitive map, Skau managed to navigate. By 0200 hours on February 22 his men had landed on the beach east of Los Banos, within a few yards of the jungle area where they would conceal themselves for the next thirty hours. The canoes were quietly dragged out of the water, pulled deep into the jungle, and carefully concealed. Then Skau and his unit went to ground.

At dawn on February 22, the engineers moved their bulldozers onto Nichols Field and set to work. They completed their task by mid-afternoon. Nine C-47 air-craft from the 65th Troop Carrier Squadron flew in with a supply of parachutes for Ringler and his men. The aircraft were then dispersed around the field and pre-pared for the drop at dawn the following morning.

During the early afternoon, Colonel Lackey, using one of his aircraft, took Lieutenant Ringler, Colonel Burgess, Colonel Gibbs, and Lieutenant Colonel La Flamme on a reconnaissance flight over Los Banos. A close look at the battlefield area was a luxury not often afforded junior commanders.

The reconnaissance flight complete, a general meet-ing was held to work out final details of the plan. The commanders then returned to their respective units and briefed their complements on the details of the operation. Ringler and Burgess warned their men that care had to be taken when attacking the camp to avoid casualties among the prisoners. Some prisoners, they knew, would be in poor health. They would need immediate attention.

As darkness fell over Paranaque, a convoy of trucks carrying La Flamme's 1st Battalion set out for the journey down Route 1 for Mamatid. Directly behind the trucks were fifty-nine amphtracs of the 672nd Bat-talion carrying Colonel Burgess and the remaining com-panies of the 1st Battalion of the 511th.

On Nichols Field, Ringler's men checked their parachutes and equipment, then unrolled their sleeping bags under the wings of the C-47s. The men preferred to sleep under the aircraft in the open rather than retreat to ramshackle buildings close to the airfield.

At 2330 hours, while most of the paratroopers slept, La Flamme's battalion set up a night camp in Mamatid. While the glidermen prepared night camp, the amphtrac drivers, with the aid of the paratroopers, lined up their vehicles near the water's edge. They were prepared to enter the water at 0500 hours.

General Swing was awakened by his orderly shortly after midnight. Following the instructions of Muller, Swing informed the general that he had received a disturbing signal from his counterpart in Air Corps intelligence. The Air Corps officer had just heard from one of his sophisticated night-reconnaissance aircraft reporting increased activity in the region of the prison camp. The crew of the reconnaissance aircraft, a P-61 "Black Widow," had observed a long column of vehicle lights passing close to the camp.

Swing discussed the situation with Muller and other members of his staff. They considered calling off the operation. But when no further reports of activity came from the reconnaissance aircraft, Swing decided to carry on as planned. (It was later discovered that when the amphtracs moved through Manila, the Japanese had mistaken them for tanks. Under cover of darkness, the Japanese then moved troops and equipment toward Mamatid, positioning them on either side of Route 1. They had assumed that the "tanks" were going to be used to take the southern region of Luzon.)

In the dense jungle near the prison camp, Skau glanced at his wristwatch. The time was 0300 hours. He ordered one group of his men to move toward the

beach, another toward the intended drop zone close to
the railway tracks that ran between the town and the
prison camp. With the remainder of his men, Skau
crawled quietly in the direction of the camp. Within a
few hours some of Skau's most skillful men came within
a few feet of the outlying machine-gun emplacements.
The remainder of his troops were close to the camp
fence, only a short distance from their assigned targets.

At 0645 hours, exactly as Peter Miles had predicted,
sleepy-eyed prisoners staggered out into the compound
and lined up for morning roll call. At the same time,
Japanese soldiers lined up in an adjacent compound,
dressed only in shorts and underwear, and began their
morning physical training exercises. Skau's men moved
in for the silent kill, slitting the throats of enemy
soldiers in the outposts.

On the lake the convoy of fifty-nine amphtracs neared
Los Banos. Leaving the beach at Mamatid, the amphtracs
headed east into the middle of the lake. They stayed
away from the lake shore to avoid detection. When the
amphtracs were directly opposite Mayondon Point, east
of Los Banos, they turned south, hoping this maneuver
would bring them to their assigned beach.

Daylight filled the sky as the sluggish amphibians
wallowed toward shore. Throttling back, the drivers
proceeded at a slow speed that made the vehicles
difficult to control. All eyes scanned the coastline for
recognizable features. None could be found.

Just thirty seconds before 0700 hours, Gibbs and
Burgess heard a hoarse cry from one of the drivers. The
man was pointing to the shoreline. Four wisps of smoke
trailed into the sky, two marking the shoreline and two,
a short distance inland, marking the drop zone. Burgess
and Gibbs looked at each other and smiled: the reconnaissance team had succeeded in one of their vital

tasks. Gibbs ordered full ahead on all vessels; as he did so, nine C-47s roared overhead at an altitude of 450 feet. When the aircraft passed, the snarling of fifty-nine amphtrac engines at full throttle drowned out all further conversation.

At exactly 0700 hours the Japanese officers started to move down the line of prisoners, conducting a head count. From his concealed observation post, Skau saw a few Japanese soldiers glance toward the trails of smoke that lingered over the beach area. A moment later, Lackey's nine C-47s roared overhead. Skau saw Ringler drop from the door not four hundred feet above the ground. The rest of the paratroopers followed in close order.

Skau glanced at the man lying beside him. The soldier's bazooka was aimed at a large gun emplacement next to the camp's main entrance. Skau gave the signal to fire. The soldier squeezed the firing lever. The projectile screamed into the gun emplacement, blowing it to pieces.

The startled Japanese soldiers, in the middle of exercises, raced toward the wall where their weapons were stacked. Most were cut down by Skau's marksmen. Those who reached their goal died with their weapons in their hands.

The prisoners dived for the ground at the first burst of gunfire. Frantically the women hustled their children back to the prison huts.

Ringler and his men had a perfect drop. Only one paratrooper was injured—knocked unconscious when his head hit the railway tracks. Within three minutes of landing, Ringler had deployed his men toward camp, where they made contact with Skau's reconnaissance. They charged the prison compound, firing as they went.

Once on the beach, amphtracs fanned out, taking light fire from hidden marksmen. The amphtracs' machine gunners responded with scathing bursts of fire. In moments, all enemy fire ceased. Skau's men jumped on the leading amphtracs to set up their guns and mortars. Guided by the reconnaissance force, the first elements of the amphibious assault made for the camp.

At Mamatid, La Flamme's battalion, now reinforced with a tank-destroyer company and two field-artillery battalions, moved rapidly south along the road. La Flamme had called for a fast pace in order to confuse the enemy. His plan was working. He received little enemy fire.

By 0720 hours the entire garrison of the prison camp, some 275 enemy soldiers, had fallen under Ringler and Skau's withering fire. Only one internee was injured in the assault: neither Ringler nor Skau had lost any men. The prisoners, overjoyed, laughed and cried as they tried to hug the soldiers who had rescued them. Ringler and Skau urged the prisoners to calm down. All 2,147 had to be organized by the time the amphtracs roared into the camp with the 511th.

The amphtracs were jammed with women, children, and disabled evacuees when they moved out toward the beaches. The drivers had orders to cross the lake to Mamatid as quickly as possible, drop the evacuees, and return to collect the remaining able-bodied evacuees.

Burgess waited for the return of the amphtracs, then called General Swing and told him to halt the galloping assault of La Flamme, who was already within five miles of Los Banos. Burgess, on the beach, received only light sniper fire. In Skau's reconnaissance unit, the Americans enjoined the aid of the Filipino guerrillas in routing out snipers. A small observation aircraft overhead confirmed to Burgess that no Japanese reinforcements were coming into the area.

When the amphtracs returned, the entire beach party scrambled aboard. Evacuees, paratroopers, reconnaissance men, guerrillas, and artillery men headed north to safety in Mamatid. Meanwhile, on Route 1, La Flamme turned his troops toward Mamatid. La Flamme's diversionary unit was the only group that suffered serious casualties: two men were killed and two wounded just before La Flamme was ordered to return. But it was a small cost to save the lives of more than two thousand innocent people. Judging from other Japanese actions, these prisoners would certainly have been slaughtered had they not been rescued in this action.

The Los Banos raid was brilliantly conceived and perfectly executed. A tactical masterpiece, it remains, to this day, a prime example of effective military planning and execution. Unfortunately, the officers and men of the 11th Airborne Division—Colonel Lackey's Troop Carrier Squadron, Colonel Gibbs's Amphibious Tractor Battalion, the Filipino guerrillas, Peter Miles, and all others involved in the operation—did not receive the acclaim they deserved. Their remarkable feat was overshadowed by another great event, the landing of the Marines on Iwo Jima. However, among military men, many will concede that Los Banos was the somewhat brighter jewel.

10

BATTLEFIELD LOG:
Sukchon, Sunchon and Munsan-ni, Korea, 1950–1951

When World War II ended, the Armed Forces of the United States were drastically reduced. One of the three airborne units that existed at the end of the war, the 101st, was removed from the active list. The two remaining airborne divisions, the 11th and the 82nd, were determined to remain on the active list by becoming elite fighting forces.

A number of senior military leaders, enthusiastic about the use of paratroopers, looked upon the airborne as a sizable fighting force that could be deployed anywhere in the world at short notice. The senior military made sure that funding was readily available for training and for development of parachutes, transport aircraft, weapons, and air-transportable vehicles and equipment.

Between 1946 and 1949 the airborne concept developed rapidly. Both the 11th and 82nd Airborne Divisions were used extensively during every major field exercise both at home and abroad. Airborne training operations and field exercises received wide publicity during those few years. As a result, the most glamorous job in the Army during that period was that of the paratrooper.

When the Korean war erupted in 1950, airborne and parachute operations, although quite far advanced, were not sufficiently developed to meet the immediate problems of the conflict. Despite heavy pressure from the nation's political leaders to send airborne divisions into Korea, General MacArthur held back, realizing an airborne assault was impractical. As a consequence, the first American troops deployed to Korea were sent by sea. MacArthur did not completely dismiss the idea of using airborne units. He requested an airborne, regimental-size combat team to be mobilized and sent to Japan to act as a reserve unit.

By September 1950 MacArthur controlled most of southern Korea. Seoul, the capital of the republic, had been recaptured from the North Koreans. As a result of the rapid advance of MacArthur's United Nations forces, eight enemy divisions were trapped in the southwestern part of the country, surrounded by American and Republic of Korea forces. MacArthur knew that it was simply a matter of time before the trapped divisions either surrendered or were annihilated by his own forces. He turned his attention to the area north of Seoul.

The enemy forces holding the city now retreated northward along the west coast toward their own capital city, Pyongyang. MacArthur formulated plans to pursue them.

The 187th Airborne Regimental Combat Team, three thousand men under the command of Colonel Frank Bowen, were sent from the United States to Japan in early September with orders to prepare for a drop close to Seoul. The drop would support the amphibious landings during the assault on the city. However, as a result of some good intelligence information, it was decided that the 187th would not be required. They were ordered to stand by as a reserve unit.

When the amphibious landings proved successful, and the immediate area around Seoul was declared secure, the 187th was transported to Kimpo Airfield, a short distance north of the city.

Meanwhile, Bowen was seeking a mission for his command. On October 10 he was instructed by headquarters to prepare for a drop on any one of six specified targets in North Korea. Headquarters also informed him that he would be given no more than four days' warning of the exact target. Bowen came away from headquarters shaking his head. He felt he needed at least two weeks' warning before an operational drop in order to train his men in the procedures used by the artillery, the communications units, the tactical air-support units, troop-carrier units, and other specialists.

MacArthur, meanwhile, was in the final stages of planning a drive northward. He wanted to surround enemy forces and block their withdrawal toward the Chinese border. For this operation MacArthur needed airborne forces that could block the enemy's line of retreat. If he allowed other elements of the United Nations ground forces to catch up with the fast-retreating North Koreans, those units could be wiped out in a single action.

On October 15, Bowen and his staff met with the senior officers of the troop carrier squadrons of the Far East Air Force. They were informed that eighty-seven aircraft would be available within a week. As the meeting wound up, Bowen received a signal from headquarters ordering him to prepare his regiment for a jump on October 20 on two road and rail junctions north of Pyongyang.

The troop-carrier commanders told Bowen that they could not possibly have all eighty-seven aircraft available by that date. The most they could supply would be seventy-nine. To further complicate the issue, the assigned aircraft were in Japan. It would require several days to get them to Kimpo. However, when Bowen discovered that the transport unit assigned to him was the 314th Troop Carrier Group, he was more confident. His regiment had trained extensively with the 314th in the States and the groups had developed a good working relationship.

Reporting to headquarters, Bowen learned that his unit was to be dropped at the towns of Sunchon and Sukchon to the north of Pyongyang. He was ordered to hold the area for approximately twenty-four hours, then start south to link up with two other United Nations units. The Australian infantry regiment would drive north through Pyongyang with a support element of American tanks. Meanwhile, a South Korean unit would advance from the mountain region east of the city.

Two roads, with railway lines alongside, run north from Pyongyang. One veers slightly to the east, passing through Sunchon, thirty-seven miles north of the city. The other veers slightly west, traversing Sukchon, thirty-five miles north of Pyongyang. The towns are approximately twelve miles apart. Between them, a small road runs almost due east and west. Bowen was ordered to allocate half his forces to one town and the remaining half to the other. When he commenced his drive south to link up with the Australians and the South Koreans, he was told to pay particular attention to the tunnels on both railway lines. Intelligence reports indicated that the North Koreans were transporting American prisoners northward by rail. According to the intelligence, the train carrying the prisoners moved only during the night, avoiding the ever-present threat of an air attack by the United Nations forces. Its progress was further slowed by a crew that had to moved ahead of the train repairing sections of damaged track. By day, trains remained hidden from marauding aircraft in the numerous tunnels that lace the Korean mountains. Not knowing the location of the prison train, headquarters insisted that all tunnels be carefully examined before they were destroyed.

Colonel E. W. Hampton, commander of the 314th Troop Carrier Group, realized that Bowen needed aircraft. Hampton obtained eighty serviceable, twin-tailed boom C-119s (Flying Boxcars) and forty C-47s from the 21st Troop Carriers Squadron. C-47s, the workhorses of the airborne during World War II, were without question the most battle-seasoned transporters in the world. However, the C-119, which was a derivative of the C-82 that had been designed and built in preparation for the invasion of Japan, was a fledgling: it had never been used in an operational combat jump.

The aircraft that arrived at Kimpo were guided into marshaling areas around the airfield. Throughout October 18 and 19 they were loaded for the drop. The C-47s were assigned to equipment and supply drops only, while the C-119s were rigged to drop a combination of men, equipment, and supplies.

Preparation and loading of the aircraft took considerably longer than Bowen had expected, primarily because his men were badly out of practice. By late in the evening of October 19, all the aircraft were ready. With the loading completed, the paratroopers tried to catch some sleep. They would rise at 0230 hours to prepare for predawn take-off. The weather, unfortunately, did not cooperate. Conditions started to deteriorate before midnight, and by 0230 hours it was pouring. The paratroopers boarded the aircraft in blinding rain. At dawn the weather worsened: it was beginning to look as though the entire operation would have to be canceled.

Bowen, in constant contact with headquarters and the weather forecasters, was informed by headquarters that the decision to abort was entirely his. Meteorologists assured him that the weather would clear by late morning. Bowen asked his men to remain in the aircraft.

Bowen's faith in his meteorologists was rewarded just before noon. As the weather cleared, the aircraft taxied to the end of the runway. The leading aircraft accelerated, shuddering under its heavy load. As the wheels lifted, the pilot eased the aircraft into a gentle climb. Behind, on the runway, the second aircraft was already in position, under full throttle. For the next thirty minutes the lift-off pattern was repeated until all aircraft were in the air.

As the lead aircraft crossed west of Kimpo, it assumed an oval, "racetrack" pattern. All the aircraft heading for the Sukchon drop zone followed the same formation. The formation that was to pass over Sunchon assumed a similar "racetrack" pattern circling steadily until all planes were aloft.

When formation was complete, the flight leaders turned west, heading over the Yellow Sea. The second flight followed the first, making one massive formation. A squadron of P-51 Mustang fighters was positioned defensively around the lumbering transporters.

For almost an hour the formation droned along with the nimble P-51s working their way up and down the long line. One hundred miles from land, the formation wheeled north for another fifty miles. Finally, they swung northeast. The leader of the second flight led his formation to one side, forming a separate echelon.

Both flight leaders concentrated on the landfalls that would lead them to their drop zones. They made careful adjustments to their headings in order to maintain accuracy. To ensure a successful drop, the transporter pilots had to pay considerable attention to wind and altitude. If the aircraft were blown downwind of the drop zone, the paratroopers would land far from their target area.

The two formations dropped to seven hundred feet when they were twenty miles from the coast. Formations of fighters and fighter bombers swept in, strafing the drop zones.

By 1420 hours three thousand paratroopers were on the ground, fifteen hundred at Sukchon and the remainder at Sunchon. Little resistance was encountered. Twenty-four tons of equipment were dropped in cargo bundles. This equipment was followed later that day with further supplies. Before darkness descended, the 187th commanded high ground surrounding the two towns. The 2nd Battalion had linked up with the South Korean forces driving in from the east. Bowen detached groups of his men to search the nearby tunnels in the hope of discovering the train carrying the American prisoners. Frightened peasants had taken shelter in the tunnels, along with several groups of enemy soldiers who were also hiding. There were a few skirmishes. But no sign of the prisoners.

On the following day, October 21, the C-119s returned with further supplies. They parachuted in four trucks, forty jeeps and trailers, four 90-mm guns, twelve 105-mm field howitzers, scores of mortars, and over 550 tons of ammunition and supplies. This was the first time a combat drop had been made with a substantial amount of heavy transport equipment and artillery pieces. Credit for the operation went to Colonel Bowen, his staff, and the pilots and men of the Air Force troop transporter squadrons.

Late that night some fierce fighting broke out as the 187th encountered the 239th North Korean Regiment, which was trapped between Pyongyang and drop zones. The battle raged throughout the night. Several 3rd Battalion posts to the south of Sukchon were almost overrun, but the battalion regrouped and, by dawn, drove the enemy back to defensive positions.

As the first dull light of dawn appeared over the horizon, the Australians, with their American tank units, mounted an attack from the south. Bowen's men started a slow push toward them, squeezing the enemy. By noon, the Australians were face to face with the men of the 187th. Around them lay the bodies of over one thousand enemy. A short distance away, almost nine hundred enemy prisoners were being escorted south to prison camps. The 239th North Korean Regiment was destroyed.

On the following day, Bowen received orders to march down the road to Pyongyang. Their task was completed. During the battles around Sunchon and Sukchon the 187th sustained a total of 111 casualties, many fewer than Bowen had anticipated.

Late in November 1950 the Chinese staged a massive counteroffensive. By January 1951 the United Nations forces had been driven back below Seoul. In April, General MacArthur was relieved of command in the Far East. In public statements he said that American forces should invade China and that "there is no substitute for victory." This stance earned him the disapproval of President Truman, who planned to negotiate a truce with the North Koreans and the Chinese.

General Matthew Ridgway replaced MacArthur. He quickly organized an offensive to recover Seoul and drive the enemy back to the north. The 1st Division of the Republic of Korea spearheaded the assault. On

March 14 and 15 the Chinese and North Koreans were driven out of the capital.

Bowen's 187th was again called to make a parachute drop. The action was similar to the one that had been carried out at Sukchon and Sunchon. He was ordered to muster his troops, along with two companies of Rangers, at Taegu Airfield, some 127 miles south of Seoul. They were to prepare for assault.

As the enemy retreated north along the road to Kaesong and Pyongyang, Ridgway ordered the 187th to drop in the vicinity of Munsan-ni, thirty miles north of Seoul. Ridgway was hoping to trap a major unit of the North Korean Army south of Munsan-ni. He intended to bring the South Korean 1st Division out of Seoul to wipe out the trapped enemy.

Bowen, with a total of 3,300 men, was allocated fifty C-119s and forty-five C-46 "Commando" transporters. A further twenty-four C-119s were assigned to deliver twenty 105-mm howitzers, twenty 90-mm guns, fifty jeeps with trailers, ten trucks, and hundreds of tons of ammunition and supplies.

Throughout March 21 and 22, the troops prepared their equipment and loaded the aircraft. Under clear, star-specked skies, the troops were marched to the waiting aircraft. As dawn broke, the C-119s lined up on the dusty runway. Visibility was down to fifty yards in the swirling dust. Taking off at ten-second intervals, the pilots had to fly "blind" through the artificial dust storm.

For the pilots these were nightmarish conditions. Swirling dust clogged the engine filters. They were losing power when they needed it most. Every pilot who went through the "blind" take-off routine breathed a sigh of relief when his aircraft broke out into the clear, blue-gray sky.

The transporters formed up over Taegu. As the last aircraft swung in at the rear of the column, the formation was joined by the familiar, nimble P-51 escort fighters. Shortly before 0900 hours a C-47 arrived high over Munsan-ni and directed scores of fighters and bombers on strafing runs over the drop zone. The C-47, an aerial command-and-control post, would remain over the drop zone, directing both transporters and the air-support elements, until the entire operation was complete.

A short distance from the area, a group of P-51s circled the tiny L-4 observation aircraft. It was a strange sight, the sleek fighters flying in wide circles around the slow-moving L-4s. At this slow speed, the P-51s were in danger of going into a stall.

The fighter pilots later discovered that the L-4 carried the theater commander, General Ridgway, who viewed the entire operation from the air. Against the protestations of his staff, Ridgway had insisted that he go in the tiny L-4. His only concession to senior staff was in allowing the craft to be escorted by a fighter group.

At 0900 hours the men of the 187th, and their guest jumpers, the Rangers, began the drop. They were just five hundred feet above the ground. For almost twenty minutes the air over Munsan-ni was filled with the droning of the lumbering transport aircraft and the snapping of parachutes opening in the morning air.

After the paratroopers landed, General Ridgway ordered his pilot to come down on a small road within the drop zone. The fighter escorts were chagrined to learn that the cargo-carrying C-119s were approaching and they would have to clear the area.

Bowen's men quickly set up roadblocks and went into defensive positions to await the drop of their heavy equipment. In the surrounding area they encountered only light resistance from isolated groups of retreating enemy. It took them only a short time to realize that no major enemy group was left in the area. Although the operation was a disappointment, Bowen was well satisfied with the performance of his regiment. General Ridgway complimented the men on their professionalism.

The drop on Munsan-ni was the second and final airborne operation in Korea. It remained the last significant airborne combat assault by American forces until the Ranger Battalions parachuted onto the island of Grenada in October 1984.

ABOUT THE AUTHOR

IAN PADDEN was born and educated in England. During service with the British Military he learned to fly and also developed an interest in specialized reconnaissance, espionage, and counter insurgency warfare. His interests in these subjects required him to have a thorough knowledge of other special ("elite") military units throughout the world.

He was taught deep-sea diving by Royal Navy instructors and worked as a commercial diver in construction, salvage, and offshore oil drilling. He spent further time in the oil industry working as a driller, drilling supervisor, and drilling engineer and was later employed by one of the world's leading subsea drilling equipment manufacturers as a specialist engineer and training instructor. He left the company to become a drilling consultant, and in that capacity has been responsible for drilling oil wells, both on land and offshore, throughout the world.

One of Ian's hobbies is aerobatic competition flying. He has been a member of the British Aerobatic Team since 1978 and has represented Great Britain in two world championships.

Ian Padden began writing in 1963 when he presented a special paper on "The Foundation, Formation and Operating Principles of the Roman Army" to the British Army School of Education. In 1965 he assisted in the writing of "The Principles of Diving" by Mark Terrell (Stanley Paul: London). During his career in the oil industry, he was commissioned to write training manuals and narrations for training films. He has also written two television scripts and various treatments for documentaries. He is currently finishing a full-length novel.

The Fighting Elite ™

AMERICA'S GREAT MILITARY UNITS

by Ian Padden

Here is the magnificent new series that brings you into the world of America's most courageous and spectacular combat forces—the Fighting Elite. Each books is an exciting account of a particular military unit—its origins and training programs, its weaponry and deployment—and lets you relive its most famous battles in tales of war and valor that will live forever. All the books include a special 8-page photo insert.

Special Offer
Buy a Bantam Book
for only 50¢.

Now you can have Bantam's catalog filled with hundreds of titles plus take advantage of our unique and exciting bonus book offer. A special offer which gives you the opportunity to purchase a Bantam book for only 50¢. Here's how!

By ordering any five books at the regular price per order, you can also choose any other single book listed (up to a $4.95 value) for just 50¢. Some restrictions do apply, but for further details why not send for Bantam's catalog of titles today!

Just send us your name and address and we will send you a catalog!